# "JUST A COUNTRY PREACHER"
# B. R. LAKIN

# "JUST A COUNTRY PREACHER"

# B. R. LAKIN

Dr. Bascom Ray Lakin
1901-1984

Second printing

# CONTENTS

# AUTHOR'S NOTE

Dr. Bascom Ray Lakin once said that he'd like to be remembered "merely as a country preacher that has never dipped his colors and never sought to advance himself. I want to be loved by the great majority of people who believe the like precious truth. I'd like to be known as a man who never wavered, never faltered."

It is said that when Abraham Lincoln died, the man who pulled the sheet over his head said, "Now he belongs to the ages." So it is with Dr. Lakin—now he is a part of the rich heritage that the great preachers have left to us.

This book is a small part of the history of B. R. Lakin. But the far larger part of Dr. Lakin is spread throughout this country in the hearts and minds of those he loved enough to lead to his Saviour, Christ Jesus. May they continue to spread the Gospel as he did and just go around "bragging on Jesus."

*Angela E. Hunt*

# FOREWORD

Dr. B. R. Lakin, without a doubt, was the "Prince of Preachers" of this century. I first met Dr. Lakin when the Thomas Road Baptist Church was a very young and growing congregation.

Throughout the past 25 years, Dr. Lakin conducted dozens of special meetings and crusades here in our home church.

Dr. and Mrs. Lakin (called affectionately "Mommie Bob" by all who know and love her) had only one child. Their son Bill was killed in an automobile accident while still a young husband and father. Dr. and Mrs. Lakin, then, symbolically adopted me as "their son" many years ago.

Our relationship has been a very intimate one. He has been my spiritual father, mentor, and close friend. His advice through the years has been precious. This man was one of the first to conduct a daily, nationwide religious broadcast. He knew all the great "spiritual giants" of the early 20th century whom I had read about and respected so highly. He often preached to thousands of people on Sunday mornings in the great Cadle Tabernacle, where he preached for many years, having been invited there by the great Howard Cadle, the Tabernacle's founder.

Dr. Lakin has, without question, contributed significantly to making America a better place in which to live. His message has changed and influenced the lives of countless Americans who have gone on to be those citizens of decency, integrity, and honor who have throughout the years taught our children, worked in our plants, fought our wars, run our businesses, and pastored our churches—citizens who are the backbone of this great America. Dr. Lakin's message has consistently been one of salvation, of patriotism, and of liberty.

He, fittingly, preached his last sermon from the pulpit of the Thomas Road Baptist Church on February 26, 1984. He was already quite ill. On March 15, 1984, lying in his bed at the Virginia Baptist Hospital in Lynchburg, Virginia, Dr. Lakin quietly went to be with his Lord. Moments earlier, he had concluded a telephone call to his dear wife who was five miles away in the Holiday Inn.

As he requested, he is buried in the beautiful Memorial Garden adjacent to the Prayer Chapel on Liberty Mountain, which is the campus of Liberty University. He was the last of his kind. He was God's gift to me. I shall cherish his memory.

*Jerry Falwell*

# Chapter 1

# FROM MOUNTAIN MEN

**Mountaineers Are Always Freemen**
*—state motto of West Virginia*

The earliest settlers of West Virginia were cabin-dwelling farmers of English, Scotch-Irish, and German descent. They were the ancestors of Bascom Ray Lakin—hardy people with a fierce pride in their rugged and individualistic ways.

The Civil War devastated the South during the 1860's, but West Virginia was largely untouched by the conflict. When the prospect of war first loomed, most Western Virginians (Virginia and West Virginia were one state at the time) were sympathetic with President Lincoln. Due to the mountainous terrain of their land, they had no great plantations and no slaves. When Virginia voted to secede from the Union, loyal West Virginians quickly voted to become an independent state.

And so West Virginia was admitted to the Union as the 35th state on June 20, 1863. Just a few years later in the small settlement on the forks of the Big Sandy River, Richard Lakin was born.

The Big Sandy River flows out of the Ohio River and provides the boundary between Kentucky and western West Virginia. At one point the Big Sandy forks into two smaller streams: one, Tug Fork, continues the West Virginia boundary and the other fork meanders off into Kentucky. But at the forks of the Big Sandy is a prosperous town of about 700 people called Fort Gay.

During the time of Richard Lakin, social gatherings in Fort Gay were much like those in other small West Virginia towns. Weddings, cornhuskings, and family reunions were popular with clan-conscious mountain people. The clans were also protective—Fort Gay was in Wayne County, scene of the famous Hatfield-McCoy feud which took place during Richard Lakin's childhood.

Bascom Ray Lakin as a seven-year-old.

Richard Lakin was a native West Virginian, born and reared about two miles from where his sons would later be born. He was a proud man, hard working and determined to owe no man anything. The Lakin name was an old name in that part of the country, and Richard felt the family pride fiercely. Folks always thought that Richard was brilliant, and his family regretted that he never had much opportunity for education or study.

But Richard was determined to do well. He knew he might never be rich or famous, but if he could provide for a family and keep his farm out of debt, he would consider himself successful.

By hard work and perseverance he met his goals. He never had a mortgage on his farm, but he worked from four a.m. until nightfall to sustain his farm and provide a comfortable living for his family. B. R. Lakin used to say, "My father had a poverty program—we all worked."

Richard Lakin was a slight man, shorter than the girl he married. He always wore a full, neatly trimmed moustache and kept his brown hair neatly clipped close to his head.

Though he didn't have much use for religion, when he was thirty years old Richard joined the Methodist Church and was sprinkled. Thirty years later he came forward during one of his son's meetings in a little country church, took his hand, and said, "Son, I always knew it was right, but my family pride kept me from doing it. I want you to baptize me." So Richard Lakin was baptized by his son in the same spot where J. C. Simpkins baptized Bascom Ray Lakin.

B. R. Lakin baptized his father, Richard Lakin, in the Big Hurricane Creek. His first pastorate was the Evangel Baptist Church, located in the tiny settlement of Greenbrier Creek. He commuted to that church on a mule and earned a monthly salary of $7.00. In his saddlebags he carried his Bible, a copy of *Pilgrim's Progress,* and his "other shirt." As he preached, he prayed, "God, lay the weight of the world upon me. Give me love for every soul for whom Jesus died. Help me preach as a dying man to dying men with a broken heart and tears."

Richard Lakin developed sugar diabetes, the same disease which would later plague his son. His feet turned black with painful polyps and the man who had walked miles behind a plow was unable to leave his bed. A few days before Richard died, Bascom Ray stood at his father's bedside and asked, "Daddy, are you afraid to die?"

"No," Richard replied. "I hate to leave your mother and you children, but I'm not afraid to die."

"What about the sting of death?" his son questioned.

"There is no sting for a Christian," Richard murmured.

Richard's influence lived on in the spirit of his son. Bascom Ray later said, "There isn't a day that passes that I don't think about my Daddy."

# Chapter 2

# MOLLIE

**"That best academy, a mother's knee"**
*—James Russell Lowell*

Mary Elizabeth was upset. Her parents had decided to move west, and the thought of leaving her home and her friends tore at the young girl's heart. She was fifteen—ready to prepare for marriage and a home of her own, but suddenly her parents had the crazy notion of moving!

She toyed with the idea of announcing her independence and offering to stay behind with relatives, but inwardly Mary Elizabeth knew that her place was with her parents. A devout Christian, she knew that children were to obey and honor their parents until they were married.

"Okay," she thought. "I'll go along with the idea. But I can't wait until I have a home of my own. I'm never going to move my family around like this."

The Farmer family loaded their belongings into wagons and moved from Tazewell County, Virginia to Greenbrier County, West Virginia. But they didn't stay there long. Before Mary Elizabeth knew what was happening, they were loading and moving again, this time to Wayne County, further west and almost to the Kentucky border.

One afternoon Mary Elizabeth was walking down the dusty road that led to their new home. Her ears were full of the conversation she had overheard in the small country store. She had picked out the names of the neighboring towns and was trying to settle them in her mind. "Let's see," she mused. "We're in Big Hurricane, and Little Hurricane is ten or twelve miles away. Louisa is a good size city and Fort Gay is where we'll have to go if we need to do any serious shopping. Mr. Miller runs the store, the Hawkins are our closest neighbors, and the Rev. Cornutte is the pastor of the Baptist church."

As she concentrated on names and places, she failed to hear the steady sound of an approaching buggy. But the driver of the buggy, Richard Lakin, could not help but notice the dark-haired, slender girl. She was new. She was beautiful.

Lakin was born in this small home in Fort Gay, West Virginia, on June 5, 1901.

That afternoon Mary Elizabeth Farmer and Richard Lakin met. It was very soon afterwards that their families were agreed—the two should marry. At age sixteen, Mary Elizabeth became two things to Richard Lakin—"Mollie" (West Virginians were fond of nicknames) and "wife." She married Richard Lakin and moved to his farm seven miles out from the forks of the Big Sandy River in Fort Gay, West Virginia.

Richard Lakin was a Methodist and Mary Elizabeth was a Baptist, but there was not enough difference between the two to cause any problems in their marriage.

Both believed in hard work, and Richard proudly worked his farm as Mary Elizabeth took care of the children that began to arrive. She bore two sons, then a daughter. Another son soon followed, then Mary Elizabeth found that she was pregnant again.

Her children were pleasant enough, but Mary Elizabeth yearned for one child who would be special—she wanted to have a son who would be a preacher. When she first felt her unborn baby begin to move, she prayed that God would give her a "preacher man."

Lakin studies his family portrait in the room where he was born.

On a hot June afternoon in 1901, Mary Elizabeth began to feel the first pangs of labor. Richard ran to get the horse and buggy to ride for the doctor; Mary Elizabeth instructed the other children to help out with the chores. She checked on the stew for supper that evening and told her daughter to take charge in the kitchen. Then she sought out some clean sheets and some fans for the bedroom.

The afternoon wore on and through her pain she heard the sound of an approaching buggy. A few minutes later Richard peered anxiously into the room and came to kneel by the side of the bed. After carefully scanning her face, he apologized for being so slow. The roads had been muddy, he explained, and the buggy had gotten stuck more than once. But the doctor had come, and everything would be alright.

Mary knew that everything would be fine, and as old Doctor York sat with her through her labor, she told him about her prayer. After a particularly hard contraction, he asked, "What names have you chosen, Mary?"

"Only one name, for it's going to be a boy. He'll be Bascom Ray Lakin."

The forks of the Big Sandy River, where Lakin grew up.

It was nine o'clock the following morning when the anxiety in the house was finally broken. The lusty cry of a baby was heard, and Bascom Ray Lakin had entered the world. The doctor gave the baby to the proud parents, washed his hands, and remarked that his fee would be five dollars.

"Five dollars," murmured Mary as she looked at her new son. "I think we got a bargain."

B. R. Lakin had fond memories of his mother's methods for raising children. "I like the way my ma used to feed us. She'd put it all on the table and say, 'Get your chairs, kids, and come on.' We started six inches from the table and when we touched, we knew we'd had enough."

"My mother never knew anything about indigestion or tonsillitis. If we ate too many green apples and took the curl, she'd pour a bottle of castor oil down us and we'd be well in a few days. If we took tonsillitis, she swabbed us out with a little coal oil. If we'd go to bed at night with a stomachache, she'd put a hot stove lid on it—I've gotten up in the morning looking like an elephant stepped on me."

A later picture of B. R. Lakin with his mother.

"She didn't know anything about calories—don't eat this, don't eat that." But Mollie knew how to serve a meal with lots of love.

Mollie Lakin never wavered in her faith that her baby boy would be a preacher. She watched Bascom Ray grow into a strapping young man, but still he didn't get saved. He was dutiful and a good son, but he seemed to be waiting for something.

Mollie always sang as she did her work on the farm. Listening from the breakfast table, Bascom Ray would see his mother gather the milk pails and head toward the barn. Her voice would stay with him long after her figure had disappeared, and the song she sang became a part of his day: "Jesus, Lover of my soul, let me to thy bosom fly."

On the February night when Bascom Ray finally ventured into the country church and gave his life to Christ, Mollie Lakin was overjoyed. She hurried home to tell Richard, who just smiled and shook his head. "I wonder what the boy will be up to now," he mused.

"Don't you worry," said Mollie. "B. R. will make you proud."

Dr. Lakin loved to tell of one time he went to visit his mother. "I lived in the little village seven miles from town and I loved to see my mother after I came home from my little meetings. That was before we had roads that I could get down to the farm in the wintertime, so I went to the livery stable and hired a horse. One day I went in the house and didn't see her, so I went through the old parlor and I heard her singing. I saw her sitting on the back porch, singing, 'How tedious and tasteless the hour when Jesus no longer I see. Sweet prospects, sweet bird and sweet flower, have all lost their sweetness to me.'"

One night after a meeting, Dr. Lakin received a phone call from his brother. He quickly drove 300 miles back to West Virginia and met his brother at the door. "I don't know whether she'll know you or not," the brother warned.

B. R. Lakin went in and knelt beside the bed of his mother. Her eyelids had been paralyzed for many years, but her weak hand reached out toward the face of her youngest son. "This is my baby boy, my preacher boy," she whispered. "Son, before you were born I prayed that you'd be my preacher boy. And when you were born, like Hannah, I dedicated you to the Lord. I've watched every night now when eight o'clock would come, I'd pray for you. I listen to you on the radio every day and every morning—great crowds everywhere come to hear you preach, and great temptations will come to you. Promise your mother that you'll go on and preach the Gospel, just like I taught it to you when you were a little boy."

The mother and her son prayed together. At the prayer's close, Mollie softly began to clap her hands and sing, "I'm going home, I'm going home to die no more."

But Mollie's strength sustained her for a few more days. Finally, Dr. Lakin received another phone call from his brother. "Mother died this morning at 2 a.m." Dr. Lakin sat on the edge of the bed and cried like a baby. His wife put her arm around him and he said, "It's the first time I've ever been without a mother. But she's up there in heaven, now, and I believe she's still asking, 'Jesus, help my baby boy preach tonight.'"

# Chapter 3

# FROM THE FORKS
# OF THE BIG SANDY

**The childhood shows the man as morning
shows the day.**
*—John Milton*

Bascom Ray, the baby boy of the family, grew up in
the community called Big Hurricane Creek. Wearing a
long skirted dress in the fashion of the day, he enrolled
in his first school under schoolmaster Jake Dawson. He
attended the little one-room school house on Queen's
Creek until fourth grade, then he moved to a two-room
school. After finishing the eighth grade, Bascom Ray
dropped out for a while to work on the farm.

Life was full of work for a country boy on a farm. The
family of eight rose before dawn, ate breakfast, and
waited for enough light to begin work in the fields.
Bascom Ray often helped his father milk the cows and
feed the animals before the sun came up. He often said,
"we worked from 'can't see 'til can't see.'"

Bascom Ray was sent to the fields when he was ten
years old. His father cut a hoe handle in two so that the
hoe was short enough for the boy to manuever, and B. R.
joined his brothers in the field. One particularly hot afternoon the boy asked his daddy, "Do you suppose Joshua's
fighting one of those battles somewhere?"

Richard Lakin paused. "Why?"

Bascom Ray wiped the sweat from his forehead.
"Because that sun hasn't moved for an hour, I know it
hasn't."

One morning after breakfast Bascom Ray and his

father went out to the fields to cut oats before the sun rose. As they waited for enough light to begin work, the son thought of something important. "Dad," Bascom Ray questioned, "Did you sow wild oats?"

"Why, no, son, why do you ask?"

Bascom Ray laughed. "Cause it looks like you're trying to slip up on them in the dark."

Dr. Lakin's parents, Richard and Mary Elizabeth Lakin, two brothers, and one sister.

Another time Bascom Ray was trying to help his daddy free a wagon loaded with timber that had become stuck in the mud. The two mules refused to budge the load and

Bascom Ray looked to his daddy to see what would happen next.

"Son," Richard said wisely, "there's two things to do in a situation like this. The first thing to do is lighten the load."

They heaved some of the timber off the wagon and then tried to urge the mules to pull the load. Nothing happened.

When he was eighteen, B. R. Lakin was saved in this little country church in Big Hurricane, West Virginia. He preached his first sermon one week later.

"What's the second thing to do, Daddy?" asked the son.

"The second thing is real important," said the father. "You kick the mule and try again."

Dr. Lakin often joked that as a boy, he had the freedom to go anywhere he pleased after his chores were done. The only place that seemed inviting, though, was his bed.

Although he was the youngest son, a full share of chores fell to Bascom Ray. But his intellectual talents soon began to manifest themselves. He was a fast talker and a slick one, and he began to do "auctioneering" at pie socials, cake walks, and cattle sales. He liked talking so much that he also began to "preach" and imitate the country preachers he knew so well. He preached funerals for the chickens and ducks and held "pretend" church meetings for the children he played with.

Many times as he was plowing the fields behind the stubborn mule, the barefoot Bascom Ray would look up at the sky and say, "Someday I'll amount to something." But what could the future hold for a mountain boy with an eighth grade education?

Big Hurricane Baptist Church as it looks today.

When he was 17 years old, Bascom Ray took a job cutting timber in the mountains for one of the many sawmills which were springing up throughout West Virginia. He was away from home, living in a little log shanty in the head of the hollow. In February, 1918, he became ill and had to go home for a few days. While he was regaining his strength and enjoying his ma's home cooking, his mother mentioned that a revival was taking place in her little Baptist church at the forks of the creek. The preacher was Jason Simpkins, a nephew of "Devil Anse" Hatfield, a leader of the bloody legendary Hatfield-McCoy feud.

Although Bascom Ray Lakin knew that he was lost

and needed to be saved, he had never tasted booze, never gambled, and had never been in jail. He had never manifested much interest in being saved, but he had heard enough country preaching to know what salvation was all about. The favorite topic of country preachers was "hell and eternity," so Bascom Ray knew what he needed to do.

Bascom Ray let two days of the revival pass without attending, but on the third day he jokingly told his mother, "I think I'll go to church tonight and get saved and become a Methodist Bishop."

She quickly replied, "I don't care what you become, just so you get saved."

Lakin walked quickly through the crisp February air until he reached the little church. He quietly took a seat in one of the hard wooden pews. The pot-bellied stove in the corner barely heated the room on that cold February night, but the warmth of the crowd filled the room and made him glad he had come. From the other side of the room he caught his mother's loving gaze and thought, "She's praying for me to get saved." After some lively singing by the group, the Reverend J. C. Simpkins stood to speak. His sermon was titled "When I see the Blood I will Pass Over You." Bascom Ray thought the sermon would never end. His heart was ready, his mind was made up. He had decided to get saved.

When the invitation was finally given, Lakin quickly stepped into the aisle and knelt at the little mourner's bench at the front of the church. He prayed, "Lord, I don't know much about being saved, but from here on in I'll trust you and if you save me, you'll never hear the end of it."

Lakin later said, "As I knelt, Jesus walked down the aisle with a crown on his head and a cross on his back and said, 'What can I do for you?' And I answered, 'Do that for me that which I cannot do for myself.' "

Lakin stood up and knew that everything was different from that moment on. He looked at his mother; her face shone with love and pride, like an angel's. As he walked home that night, he chose to walk alone. He thought that the stars looked as though they had been washed with all the purity of God's holiness, and the trees seemed to bow down their heads and say, "We're glad." He walked over the little red clay hills and sang, "Hallelujah, 'Tis done. I believe on the Son. I'm saved by the blood of the crucified One." It was February 12, 1918—a date Bascom Ray would never forget.

Dr. Lakin had rich memories of his childhood in West Virginia. In this picture taken during his later years he stands at the site where he was baptized as a teenager.

B. R. felt as if the "Lord leaned out over heaven and dropped a chunk of salvation that hit me in the left side of the soul and turned over a whole tub of honey that'll be oozing out between my ribs for years."

On the following Sunday, Rev. Simpkins had a hole

cut through the ice in the Big Hurricane Creek. Together he and Bascom Ray stepped into the frigid waters and Lakin was baptized.

Just one week after he was saved, Bascom Ray preached his first sermon in that same little church in Big Hurricane, West Virginia. He chose John 1:29 for his text: "Behold the Lamb of God, which taketh away the sin of the world." The young preacher quickly overcame his nervousness and found that preaching to a congregation was not much more difficult than preaching to the farm animals. But he found that his text ran out in a quick 12 minutes. He'd have to think of more to say the next time.

The "next time" ran into a long series of messages. Bascom Ray Lakin, once begun, planned never to stop telling people what God had done for him and what He could do for them. From that little pine mourner's bench he rose resolved to tell the story, always "going around bragging on Jesus."

But he knew he had a lot to learn. Young Lakin had an insatiable desire to learn, read, and learn more. He did not have much opportunity for formal education, but he seized every opportunity to learn. "There may be some excuse for you being born dumb, but God knows there's no excuse for you remaining so," he believed.

Bascom Ray held his first independent meeting a few weeks later in a little church on Little Hurricane (Bascom Ray was from Big Hurricane). He carried his lantern and walked over the hills to the little log church, anticipating the warmth of the coal oil lamps and the pot-bellied stove inside. The church was a Protestant-Methodist church, and in it Bascom Ray found an eager congregation.

And so began the trail. The preacher who would later routinely cross America by jet began by walking over the mountains by lamplight.

# Chapter 4

# "Bob"

**"I only had one sweetheart."**   *—B. R. Lakin*

Bascom Ray Lakin grew up just seven miles from where Violet Crabtree was living. When young Bascom Ray was just learning to train his voice by auctioneering at pie socials and cake walks, he noticed a pretty girl in a pink dress. She shyly smiled at him, and the love affair which has never ended began.

Mrs. Lakin later said, "Oh, I knew who he was all along. I just thought that I'd watch out for that young man."

Bascom Ray had never been interested in any other girl. He kept his eye on her as they grew up, and he always knew in the back of his mind that someday he'd marry Violet Crabtree.

Then B. R. got saved and began preaching. His first series of revival meetings was held at Tabor's Creek Baptist Church. Violet was in the congregation, and B. R. was thrilled when he saw her come forward at the invitation.

The pastor of Tabor's Creek Church invited young Lakin to assist with the baptisms the following Sunday. To limit the amount of time that people had to stand in the cold creek water, the candidates for baptism were divided into two groups. Violet quietly stepped into her pastor's group, but when he spied her he remarked loudly, "Violet, I believe Bass wants you in his line." Violet blushed and Bascom Ray was embarrassed, but Violet obeyed and was baptized by B. R. Lakin.

Violet Crabtree, who later became Mrs. Bascom
Ray Lakin.

Not long afterward they began courting and, although
B. R. loved to be out preaching with Brother Simpkins,
he also looked forward to returning home. He bought a
buggy for his trips and found that it was also just right

for courting. Courtships didn't last long in those days. Bascom Ray and Violet realized that they made a good team and they could help each other. Marriage just seemed natural and right.

They were married and happily settled. Violet taught school; B. R. preached. Soon William Ashley Lakin was born, and Violet was proud and happy to be a mother. But, as usual, her practical nature enabled her to continue to work to help support their family. She was, even by modern standards, a thoroughly independent woman. Mentally tough, physically strong, and spiritually complete, circumstances just couldn't get her down.

Mrs. Lakin's birthplace near Fort Gay, West Virginia.

Through the years of Dr. Lakin's ministry, she either kept the home fires burning to welcome him or she was at his side. She was more than a wife and mother—she was Dr. Lakin's advisor, secretary, co-worker, friend, and staunchest defender.

Dr. Lakin often went for months without ever spending more than three or four days at home. But Mrs. Lakin never complained. Dr. Lakin praised her, "My wife has never said, 'Honey, you ought to be home.' She's never complained. Thank God for her. She's been the strong crutch under my arm, my right arm, through all these years, because when I got saved, He said, 'He that is not willing to forsake father and mother, husband or wife, houses and land, is not worthy of being my disciple.'"

Violet Lakin's tough upbringing and unflappable nerves brought her through more than one difficult situation with B. R. Lakin. After his first heart attack, Dr. Lakin called her from a hospital emergency room.

"Honey, they think I've had a heart attack."

Mrs. Lakin quietly soothed him. "Oh, I'm sure it is nothing so bad. Just relax and you'll be fine. I'll call again in the morning."

Mrs. Lakin hung up the phone and quickly called one of her friends in the town where Lakin happened to be preaching. "They say Lakin's had a heart attack. Can you go check on him and let me know how serious it really is?"

Mrs. Lakin later found out that it really was a heart attack and that her husband was in the intensive care unit. "Well, they are doing more for him there than I can do. Let me know when he can travel and I'll come up and get him." Few women would have the strength to take long-distance calamity so graciously.

One of Mrs. Lakin's favorite stories involves her "$1,000 doll" which is displayed on a table in her living room. The doll, a lovely ceramic lady, wears a red dress trimmed in pure gold.

Lakin went every year to a camp meeting for a week over in Missouri. The man who started the work began it without a penny—just faith in God. He had been leading a little church, no bigger than most people's living room, and he said that the Lord told him to go out and start a tabernacle. As he walked down a road one day with only ten cents in his pocket, a man drove up in a big car and asked, "What are you doing?"

"Well," the pastor said, "I'm fixing to build a church."

"Have you got any money?" asked the stranger.

"No," replied the pastor, "but God's going to give it to me."

"Well," the stranger murmured, "The Lord told me to get in my car and go find a man who was going to build a church." The stranger then handed the pastor a check for $1,500.00.

The work was begun and it thrived. Dr. Lakin would attend each year and every time, without any advertisement whatsoever, the word would spread and the crowds would pack the buildings to hear B. R. Lakin.

One thing that marked the people of this tabernacle

was a generous spirit. The people built a dining hall and prepared three meals a day for anyone who needed food—free of charge. Women would donate quilts and needlework so that they could be sold to support the tabernacle, and men freely donated their labor and skills to construct and administrate the programs.

B. R. Lakin preached his first revival meeting at the Tabor's Creek Baptist Church. Under his preaching, Violet Crabtree was saved. The young school teacher was later baptized by the evangelist, and not long afterwards, they were married. Dr. Lakin called her "Bobbie," and credited her as being the mainstay and support of his ministry.

One night while the Lakins were there, a lady brought five beautiful porcelain dolls, each painted a different color, but with each dress trimmed in pure gold. She said, "God told me to bring these dolls for the work."

The pastor said, "Well, what do you think they're worth?"

She only hesitated a second. "I think they're worth $1,000 each—that's what God wants me to sell them for."

The pastor doubted. "Well, if you think you can get $1,000 for them, you're welcome to try."

A man quickly stood. "I'll take one for my wife." Another man jumped up. "I'll give $400 for one for Mrs. Lakin."

Mrs. Lakin grimaced. "I don't particularly want one because they are so fragile and I'm traveling by plane." But another man stood and announced, "I'll pay the remaining $600 so Mrs. Lakin can have one."

The pastor called Mrs. Lakin to pick out her doll; she hesitantly chose a red one. "This is a real problem," she explained to a lady standing nearby. "I don't know how I'm going to get it home. It's so fragile!"

The lady quickly assured her. "We have a boy here who works in a packing house. I'll send him over to your hotel later and he'll box that doll for you."

He did, and the 12-inch doll was soon snugly nestled amid paper shavings and sturdy cardboard restraints. But as they boarded the plane, Mrs. Lakin was still worried. The stewardess tried to fit the box in the overhead compartment, but it was too big. Neither would it fit underneath the seat. "Listen," B. R. told the stewardess, "We're ready to take off and there's an empty seat between Mrs. Lakin and me. Why don't we just set her down there and let her ride like a lady?"

And so the $1,000 doll rode safely home, held firmly by a safety belt. Now she graces the coffee table in the Lakins' living room, forever a reminder of the faith and generosity of the people of God.

# Chapter 5

# PREACHING
# WITH POWER

**Preach not because you have to say something, but because you have something to say.**—*Richard Whately*

Those who knew him best say that there were three Lakins: the public Lakin, the dinner-table Lakin, and the private Lakin. As with most public figures, B. R. Lakin began to realize that he was living in the proverbial goldfish bowl. As he preached and traveled and achieved a degree of eminence in the West Virginia mountains, he realized that people were carefully watching him. As a preacher of the Gospel, he felt a tremendous responsibility to uphold the reputation of Christ, and he zealously guarded his public image of theologian and speaker.

Bascom Ray Lakin used the years he had spent practicing on the ducks and the chickens to good advantage. The voice which used to resound loudly at auctions and cake walks now reverberated from the halls of churches and even the sides of the mountains themselves.

His preaching style was unique. He used down-to-earth country illustrations but managed to combine them with lofty language. His pleas were eloquent and emotional. He talked about Jesus as if he were talking about his best friend. When he described Heaven, his face would fill with wonder. When he described Hell, his voice would vibrate with urgency and loathing. When he mentioned Calvary, his words were filled with tenderness and love.

Lakin would often joke "I'm uneducated, but my wife's an English teacher so she keeps me straight," but he had a great command of language. His vocabulary was precise and well-developed, but never so imposing that his message could not penetrate to the simple man. His ability from the pulpit to move and motivate people with the simple, yet profound Gospel, was one of his greatest strengths.

He was a hard-driving preacher who wasted no words and wasn't afraid to call sin by its rightful name. "Listen to me tonight," he would implore. "The man who tells you about your sin is the man that loves you. The preacher that won't tell you about your sin, the preacher that won't warn you about what's coming out yonder doesn't care for you. It's your money he's after."

Wherever he appeared, Lakin felt impelled to preach the Gospel. He let people know "God has warned some of you, but you haven't profited by the warning. He warned some of you by his servants. He said, 'I place you a watchman upon Zion's wall. If you see the sword coming and fail to warn my people, their blood will I require at your hands.' Listen tonight, God said, 'I sent my prophets and my preachers to warn you.' Listen tonight, preachers, if you're not faithful in warning your people, their blood's going to be upon your hands. I'm going to tell you this, my brother, as far as I'm concerned, your blood will never drip from these fingers because I'm going to faithfully warn you of death, and of judgment, and of hell and eternity."

Lakin always exhorted young preachers to "preach the Gospel. Stay away from preaching only about short skirts, long hair, and cigarettes." But Lakin had his own comments about those topics, too:

"A preacher once said to me, 'Don't you think that woman's skirt is too short?' I replied, 'I don't know—what color was her hair?' He didn't know—he hadn't looked that far. You can shave a man until he's as bald as Yul Brynner and put skirts that drag the ground on the women and go straight to hell. Salvation is the key."

"A man asked me, 'Can I go to heaven and smoke cigarettes?' and I said, 'Yeah, and a lot quicker.' Once a man was sitting on a plane and the woman next to him pulled out a pack of cigarettes and started to blow smoke on him. He said, 'Lady, you smoke. I chew. You can blow smoke on me if I can spit on you.' "

"But that's not the Gospel—the Gospel is how Christ died for our sins according to Scripture. Many a church has been torn up by not preaching the Gospel, but by meddlin'."

The public Lakin didn't meddle, but the dinner-table Lakin sure did. When off the Gospel platform but still under scrutiny by others, Lakin became a fun-loving jokester who didn't seem to have a serious thought in his head. He'd tell outrageous stories about life in the mountains or he'd tease children, "You'd better clean your plate or I'll smear that food into your hair." He'd tell a joke and then laugh until the tears ran down his face at his own silliness. He loved life, and the dinner-table Lakin displayed joy at its fullest.

Few people ever saw the private Lakin. Bill Pennell, one of the young preachers Lakin privately taught, said that Lakin would sit for hours discussing scripture and deep theological truths. Lakin would occasionally invite another preacher to join in private prayer, and, according to Pennell, "He prayed privately like no other man I've ever heard. You could feel the presence of the Lord and you were almost afraid to open your eyes."

As careful as he was to preach the Gospel, Dr. Lakin knew that he wasn't perfect. He openly confessed, "The sin I have to confess the most often is the sin of prayerlessness. We all need to cultivate the habit of secret prayer. Preachers pray a lot in public, but I don't think God really pays much attention to those prayers—if so, there have been enough prayers to 'save the world' to have done it by now. Prayer isn't prayer until the Holy Spirit begins the prayer. When you enter into your closet and pray in secret, then you will be rewarded openly."

Lakin learned to believe in prayer through the example of the others around him. His mother's prayers stood as a shining example of faith and conviction, and the simple, honest prayers of the people around him touched him deeply.

"I remember when I first got saved, I prayed. Yonder on the farm, I prayed in every fence corner, in every stall or stable in the barn, at the end of every corn row, and when I plowed the mule around the rocky hillside. Oh,

I didn't have much to pray about, but I remember once leaning between the plow handles and saying, 'Lord, I'll never have much education because I don't believe in it. And I'll never have any money to give you. But I tell you what I will do—I'll work hard for you.'"

When he was twenty-five Lakin learned the truth of "All things are possible to him that believeth." In Logan, West Virginia, he had been preaching at morning services for a week. One morning a lady stood up and said, "I want you to pray for Jim, my husband."

Lakin knew that Jim was a big, husky railroad engineer who worked nights, so after the service he asked when Jim would be awake in the morning. The next day after his meeting, B. R. went down to Jim's little white cottage. He walked up on the porch, and through the screen door he could see big Jim sitting in an overstuffed chair, his head bowed and his arms folded. Jim's wife was kneeling on the floor at his feet. With tears streaming down her face, she was pleading, "Jim, honey, I'm going to just die if you don't get saved."

That night, big Jim stayed home from work and attended Lakin's meeting. When the invitation was given, Jim walked down the aisle, his little wife beside him. "He fell at that altar like a sack of sand," Lakin recalled.

In town after town, meeting after meeting, B. R. Lakin saw people burdened for loved ones. He watched them pray, and later rejoice when their husbands and wives, sons and daughters were gloriously saved. When miracles like these don't occur, Lakin believed, people just aren't "touching the hem of the garment."

# Chapter 6

# Marriage: A Working Partnership

**An old bachelor is a fellow who never made the same mistake once.**
*—B. R. Lakin*

Though he often made jokes about marriage, B. R. Lakin happily married his one and only sweetheart— Violet Crabtree. She was "Bob" to him, and when they were married on August 30, 1922, Violet had no idea of what she was getting into. But, though she was only nineteen, she was a strong woman, used to handling a schoolhouse full of rowdy children. She knew she could handle anything Bascom Ray threw her way.

She was more than wife and mother; she was Dr. Lakin's secretary, advisor, correspondence clerk, accountant, and booking agent. During the many years that Dr. Lakin was away preaching, often for months at a time, Mrs. Lakin taught school, sold real estate, or whatever she could to help. Not once during all those years did she tell her husband that he should be at home. She knew what he was called to do; she was called to help him do it.

Mrs. Lakin liked to joke, "I never had to worry about B. R. and other women—he knew he had the best looking woman around."

The Lakins were a unique couple. Don Norman, who had the opportunity to know and travel with them many times over the years, marvelled at their relationship. "Mrs. Lakin gave as much to the ministry as Dr. Lakin because he was gone all the time and she did everything at home. She was very independent, yet when he was

The Lakins' log home in West Virginia.

around, she was very dependent—and it's not always easy for that to happen. They understood each other in a unique way. They respected each other's opinion and I've never seen them have an argument."

"Mommie Bob" served as wife, advisor, co-worker, and friend.

"Sometimes Dr. Lakin would overstate something and she'd say, 'Now B. R., that's not right.' But he'd firmly say, 'Now Bob, you just don't know about this.' But they had a working relationship of over fifty years. She was really his strength—before anybody else he would consult her. She was a real spiritual strength and she had a lot of insights into a lot of things. B. R. knew that, and he depended on her more than any of us will ever know."

The Lakins spent many years together in Christian service. They co-labored for the cause of Christ without weighing the cost.

# Chapter 7

# THE TRAIL BEGINS

**Well begun is half done.** —*Horace*

The tiny church in Little Hurricane, West Virginia, where B. R. Lakin preached his first meeting was made of rough logs and lit by a few coal oil lamps. Four rough-hewn steps, carved from a mountain quarry, led up to the church door. It was not an imposing place, but Bascom Ray didn't mind. There were people waiting inside, people who wanted to hear his message. He couldn't wait to get inside and "brag on Jesus some more."

B. R. soon became pastor of the Evangel Baptist Church in the small settlement of Greenbrier Creek. His church was ten miles from his home, over the mountains. Bascom Ray borrowed the family mule, Old Beck, and once a month he donned his spurs and grabbed his saddle-bags to ride Beck over the mountains to preach to his congregation in the little country church. In his saddlebags he carried his Bible, a copy of *Pilgrim's Progress,* and his "other shirt." He later recalled, "I think we had eighteen, and that must have been rally day." The small size of the church didn't bother Lakin for as he preached, he prayed, "God, lay the weight of the world upon me. Give me love for every soul for whom Jesus died. Help me preach as a dying man to dying men with a broken heart and tears." His salary was seven dollars a month.

"I put my mule in a different barn every night and

slept in the spare room. If you haven't slept in a spare room when it's four below zero, then you ain't slept. Way up in the northeast corner where it's four below zero and they haven't had any fire since time began, you get in between starched sheets and shiver, and about the time you get warmed up so you can sleep, the old deacon's hollering that it's time for you to get up. I come down stairs and he'd been sleeping with the only fire there was. He said, 'Brother Lakin, it's a lot healthier to sleep away from the fire.' I said, 'Deacon, if you don't mind, I'd rather not be quite so healthy.' "

Dr. Lakin was one of the first preachers to travel in his own private plane. Here he is being greeted by the pastor of the First Baptist Church in Kenova, West Virginia.

Years later, when he was in his eighties, Dr. Lakin received an interesting letter: "I got a letter from a man whose father was a country merchant where I held my first meeting and I stayed in their home for a week. He wrote me and said, 'When you stayed in our home, I was a boy. And I slept with you in the spare room.' "

While living in Fort Gay, B. R. Lakin became concerned because although "the town wasn't too bad, we just couldn't get any law enforcement." Lakin said, "If the old judge resigns, I'll take it." Lakin became mayor and judge, found a young policeman who was willing to make arrests, and together they cleaned up the town. When Fort Gay was "cleaned up," Lakin quit.

Bascom Ray pastored the tiny Evangel Baptist Church for a year, then he pastored the First Baptist Church of

Dr. Lakin drew crowds of thousands, but he shared his heart with the small congregations, never turning down a meeting because a church was too small.

Ceredo, West Virginia. By this time he had finished his high school education and married Violet.

"When we got married she said, 'Now, you won't want to bother your mind with the minor problems. I'll take care of all of those and just leave you for the major problems.' We've been married for sixty years and haven't had a major problem."

But life did contain some major problems and difficult situations. B. R. soon left the small church at Ceredo and felt that the Lord was calling him to something new. "Maybe I ought to go to seminary," he told his wife. "Maybe this country preacher needs to get some education."

It was a difficult time for Violet, struggling with the nausea of a first pregnancy. They returned to Fort Gay in time for the November 12, 1923, birth of William Ashley Lakin, named after evangelist Billy Sunday. Surprisingly enough, Violet's mother had just had a baby six days before William's arrival.

While B. R. waited to decide about seminary, Violet knew that someone would have to support the family so she left her new baby at home with her mother and took a part-time teaching position at a little country school a few miles away. Mrs. Crabtree nursed little William and her new baby while Violet trudged through snow and mud over the mountains to her school.

B. R.'s indecision was soon over. The First Baptist Church of Louisa, Kentucky, called him as pastor, and Lakin prayed, then accepted the call. Louisa was only seven miles from Fort Gay, so the Lakins continued to live in their hometown.

Bascom Ray often held evangelistic meetings during the week while pastoring. His successful preaching was noised about the coal camps along Pond Creek, West Virginia. He had been preaching for nine years and was only 28 years old, but his reputation had grown. The folks of Wayne County reported that "he could really preach," and the religious, the skeptics, and the merely curious came out in droves to hear the young man.

A small nine-year-old boy sat on the hard wooden pew in his little church, eager to hear the famous preacher. The service had started; they had sung the first song and had prayer. During the second verse of the next hymn, down the aisle came a hulking figure wearing a ten gallon Texas hat and carrying an oversized overcoat and big Bible. He was a mountaineer down to his boots, complete with spats.

After young Lakin was introduced, off came his coat,

off came his tie, and he took a moment to very deliberately roll up his sleeves. Like a master surgeon he was going to work.

He began by telling one story after another. He was so entertaining, was this preaching? Suddenly he roared like a passenger train, right down the rail, with fast-paced preaching, spitting out each word like a bullet, accenting each syllable clearly.

How he preached! He seemed to have the burden of the world on his shoulders. His eyes would glisten with tears and his voice would break in earnestness. He knew just what to say to move a congregation to laughter, to tears, to action. And the people responded. Hundreds were saved in small rural towns.

Walter McNeil, the small boy who heard Lakin preach in 1929, reported that in his community Lakin was such a sensation that the "colored brethren" asked if he would come to their church. Lakin was happy to preach for them and arranged for a joint service on a Sunday afternoon between the black and white churches. McNeil remembered, "There we were, blacks and whites in one great worship service in the coal camp...and Webster had not yet invented the word 'integration.'"

Lakin became extremely popular in his home state. He knew how to move people and how to charm them, but he was still just a country man at heart. Some people tried to talk him into a life of politics; he was assured a seat in the legislature if he would make himself available at the polls. But Lakin declined. His mission in life was simply to "preach the Gospel," nothing else.

After two years in Louisa, B. R. Lakin took a church in Prestonsburg, Kentucky—the Irene Cole Memorial Baptist Church. In 1937, he accepted the pastorate of the Euclid Avenue Baptist Church in Bristol, Virginia. "I went there when they had seventeen in the Sunday night service and 101 in Sunday school. I stayed almost two years, I guess, but in nineteen months, we had 400 additions to the church. The Sunday school went from 101 to nearly 800. The Sunday night service went from 17 to an overflow area in the basement. We had to install speakers in the basement to take care of the overflow crowd."

One week Dr. Lakin went up to Moody Bible Institute

to attend Founder's Week (he had attended Moody for a short time before he was married). While en route to Chicago, he and a Christian lawyer from Murfreesboro were snowbound in Indianapolis. The lawyer knew

B. R. Lakin attended Moody Bible Institute. He also received several honorary doctoral degrees: the Doctor of Divinity from Bob Jones University, the Doctor of Letters from Kletzing College, and the Doctor of Divinity from Mount Vernon University.

Howard Cadle, so he suggested that they get up early the next morning to go to the radio studio for Cadle's 6 a.m. broadcast. When Cadle was done, the lawyer introduced young B. R. Lakin and said, "Cadle, I've got a man here you need."

Cadle immediately invited Lakin to preach in his camp meeting. Lakin agreed, and as he returned home from the successful meeting, he found a letter waiting from Howard Cadle: "I'd like you to come back again next Sunday and preach for me." Dr. Lakin agreed, and after the service, Cadle managed to maneuver the country preacher into a quiet office.

"Would you consider coming here as my associate? I've been looking for a man for nine years." Lakin promised to pray about it.

# Chapter 8

# THE FAMILY GROWS

**Blessings on thee, little man,**
**Barefoot boy, with cheek of tan.**

*—J. G. Whittier*

When William Ashley Lakin was born on November 12, 1923, his parents were overjoyed. Dr. Lakin named his son after the famous evangelist Billy Sunday and he prayed that his boy would grow up to be a fine Christian man. Mrs. Lakin prayed that he'd have curly hair. "I was disappointed—I want a curly-headed baby and he had straight hair. I said, 'Well—I can't send him back, but I want a curly-headed baby.'"

A few months after that, Mrs. Lakin reported, "His hair curled—it just laid in waves. I believe with all my heart that he had the prettiest hair that I ever saw anybody have."

Little Bill Lakin grew up in the same small town of West Virginia that his parents and grandparents did. After he accepted the Lord, he requested to be baptized in the same creek as his father and grandfather. As his mother dressed him for baptism, she warned him that he would be the only one in the cold water of the creek— everyone else was going to wait for warmer weather. But Bill Lakin insisted—so he was baptized in the waters of the mountain creek just like his father and grandfather before him.

Bill was a brilliant student who attended Greenbrier Military Academy after graduation from high school and learned the importance of freedom. His parents weren't surprised when he volunteered for the Navy during World War II.

After his service on the *U. S. Stevens* during World War II, he returned home to his parents in Fort Gay. He

Bill Lakin wanted to be baptized in the same creek as his father and grandfather, B. R. was happy to oblige.

met and married Cathy—a lovely girl with brown hair and a sweet disposition who reminded him of his mother.

Not long after his marriage, Bill approached his parents with his eyes shining. Good news—a grandchild was on the way. The Lakins were never happier than when Ronnie Lakin was born.

When B. R. and Violet began to work at the Cadle Tabernacle, Ronnie and his family also moved to Indianapolis. Bill bought a motel and restaurant and managed it with a keen business sense inherited from his mother.

As much as B. R. loved his son, he believed that Bill was called to preach and ought to get down to business doing it. B. R. secretly hoped that Bill would carry on his work at Cadle Tabernacle, but Bill didn't seem to have any inclinations toward preaching. B. R. decided to wait and see what God would do.

Bill Lakin's first school picture.

The joyful preacher and his son.

During the Indianapolis years, Bill and his father were perhaps more attached than they had been for years. Bill would often drive his father to the airport for an evangelistic trip, always urging him to be careful and hurry home.

When Dr. Lakin felt called to leave the Cadle Tabernacle for another ministry, Bill still had not expressed any interest in preaching. He was 29 and quite independent when he heard that his father was resigning from the Cadle Tabernacle. "Well Dad," he said, "I'll sell the motel and Cathy, Ronnie and I will go with you." Dr. Lakin didn't attempt to dissuade him. If Bill wanted to come along to Florida, what father could protest?

Bill moved to Titusville with his parents and set up his own household. He entered the construction business and began to enjoy life in the booming Florida area. But he began to experience health problems. The doctors felt that he had a heart condition and his parents were concerned. "Don't worry," he joked. "We Lakins are tough."

Chapter 9

# Cadle Tabernacle

**What in me is dark,
Illumine; what is low, raise and support;
That to the height of this great argument
I may assert Eternal Providence,
And justify the ways of God to men.**
*—John Milton*

B. R. Lakin felt that it was the Lord's will that he leave Bristol to work with Howard Cadle, the layman who pastored the Cadle Tabernacle in Indianapolis, Indiana. He didn't exactly understand why God wanted him to leave his thriving church, but he was willing to go play "second fiddle" to Howard Cadle, that lay preacher who won every ounce of Lakin's respect. Lakin served as associate pastor for two years, but upon the death of Mr. Cadle in 1942, B. R. Lakin assumed the full pastorate of the Tabernacle.

"When I went to be his associate, I told him, 'Now you are the boss. This is your baby. And whatever you tell me to do, I'll do—even if you tell me to blow up the Tabernacle.' "

Cadle liked Lakin's attitude, but he failed to see how cunning B. R. could be. "He'd come out and we'd ride together," Lakin remembered, "and I'd say, 'You know, boss man, I believe if we would do so and so, it would be a good thing.' Cadle would say, 'You think so?' But I'd drop it there and never say another word."

"About two weeks later we'd be out riding again and I'd say, 'You know, boss, I've been thinking about what you suggested the other day. I think you've got a bright idea there.' Cadle would say, 'You think so? Well, just do 'er if you want to.' and I'd smile and say, 'Okay.' "

"In those days we were as prominent as Lum and Abner and Amos and Andy—we were celebrities. We'd go to the big meetings in the football fields and the fairgrounds, and I carried his grip, I carried his coat, and I carried his hat. When he had finished preaching, I'd go get his coat and put it on him. I believe that he that humbleth himself shall be exalted."

"I was riding down the road the other day with a young preacher, a little two-by-squirt, and he said, 'Don't you think I have the ability to build the biggest church

Dr. Lakin's travels carried him over 50,000 miles a year and during an average week he would speak to 4,000 people.

in the world?' and I said, 'No, I don't. Why don't you get over trying to be a big man. God isn't using big men, God is using little men."

Howard Cadle had begun the first daily religious coast-to-coast radio broadcast in America. (Charles Fuller had the Old Fashioned Revival Hour, but it was a weekly program.) Into this program stepped B. R. Lakin, and the uneducated country preacher was heard every day on national radio with "The Nation's Family Prayer Period." He bought time on a radio station in Cincinnati, WLW, which at that time had 500,000 watts of power—illegal today. Lakin liked to joke that he could breathe in Cincinnati and they could hear him in California. After a ruling of the Federal Communications Commission reduced the station's power to 50,000 kilowatts, the Mutual Broadcasting Corporation added his program and Lakin found that he had become the radio pastor of millions.

The Cadle years took their toll on the physical body of B. R. Lakin. He never said "no," he literally worked

In 1939, Dr. and Mrs. Lakin accepted the call of the Cadle Tabernacle. Dr. Lakin served as associate pastor for two years and immediately assumed full pastorate responsibilities when Dr. Cadle died in 1942.

two jobs, on the go night and day. He spent Sundays and Wednesdays at Cadle, but all other nights he drove to hold an evangelistic meeting at another church. Mrs. Lakin recalls, "Often he'd come in at 1 or 2 a.m., and then he'd be up every morning for the 6 a.m. radio broadcast." His work was hard, but he never complained or turned down an opportunity to share the Gospel.

Other pastors used to complain that by joining Cadle Tabernacle, Lakin had become "interdenominational." To that argument, Lakin always replied, "It was no denomination at all, there was no church there. It was just a big preaching center." When he was asked if he baptized people at the Tabernacle, he replied, "Sure." But what'd he baptize them into? "Same thing Phillip did the Eunuch."

On the 28th anniversary of Cadle Tabernacle in 1949, a special songbook was published which featured the motto of the church: "No creed but Christ... no law but love... no book but the Bible!"

The exterior of Cadle Tabernacle in Indianapolis, Indiana.

The reputation of Bascom Ray Lakin spread throughout Christians in America. He was respected and revered, something the mountain preacher never expected. On June 1, 1949, Lakin was awarded an honorary degree of Doctor of Divinity from Bob Jones University, and in November, 1950, he received an honorary Doctor of Laws degree from Kletzing College. Mary Elizabeth Lakin's preacher boy was now Dr. B. R. Lakin, but he never touted his title. He never expected or wanted to be anything more than a simple country preacher.

To B. R. Lakin, all churches were alike. When he received an invitation to preach, he never asked how large his crowd would be. He was not a respecter of preachers or persons or sizes of congregations—he'd preach to a church of 10,000 in Akron just as quickly as he'd preach to a little church of 50 up in the hills. Once a young preacher told him, "Dr. Lakin, I can't wait until my church is big enough to have you."

"Son," Dr. Lakin replied, "If you wait until you're big enough, you won't need me."

The people of Cadle Tabernacle became well known throughout the United States. Buford Cadle was known as "our genial and efficient radio announcer" and his cheerful voice opened the Nation's Family Prayer Period each morning for years. The Dixie Four Quartet sang on the radio program and attracted thousands whenever they sang in "song fests" throughout the country. Their leader, Gene Lowrey, was also the tabernacle song leader and director of the 1400 voice Cadle Choir. And Mrs. Howard Cadle remained active in her husband's ministry after his death. She also addressed the radio microphone during the Nation's Family Prayer Period, and she wrote a monthly column in *The Cadle Call,* the publication of the Cadle ministries.

*The Cadle Call* also featured a "Letters from Listeners" column in which people from across the nation wrote to share what the radio broadcast meant to them. One letter, published in March, 1951 praised the wit and wisdom of B. R. Lakin:

When your program was over last Sunday, I was speechless, for I never heard such words fall from the lips of mortal man, and with the spirit of the Holy Ghost in it, as you preached that day. Oh how thankful I am for men like you, that are not afraid of what people say, but think more of what Jesus would say. You have a voice that carries the message you bring right into the heart of all of us. Even my maid comes in of a morning, wanting to know if I heard Mr. Lakin this morning, and nearly all the time I say yes, but if I do have to miss, she will say he was wonderful this morning. It isn't you, as you will agree, but it is you allowing the Lord to use you....

In the late 1940's, a young man called Billy Graham preached one of his first national sermons at the Cadle Tabernacle. After young Graham finished, Lakin muttered to himself, "I have an idea that young fellow may just go somewhere." Lakin gave the young preacher a love offering of $4,800 and prayed that he would do well.

Lakin stayed in Indianapolis for fourteen years. During that time, crowds of over 5,000 often poured into the unique Tabernacle building to hear the country preacher. He felt honored to be the preacher/pastor of the Cadle Tabernacle. His foreword in the 28th anniversary songbook says, "I know of no institution in America that has stood like a mighty Gibraltar of fundamental evangelism as has Cadle Tabernacle. This great Gospel center has never dipped its colors, but has always stood true to the fundamentals of the Christian faith."

The usual crowd at Cadle Tabernacle.

In 1952, Dr. Lakin resigned his leadership of the Cadle Tabernacle and moved to Florida to take up full time evangelistic work. It was the last time he pastored, but his greatest days were still ahead. But, Dr. Lakin always said that Howard Cadle was one of the greatest and godliest men he ever knew. He often credited Mr. Cadle with giving him his "big" opportunity to speak to the world.

James Deweerd succeeded Lakin at the Tabernacle, then later someone else assumed leadership. But the great days were over. There were no more Lakins or Cadles to bring in the crowds. The Tabernacle was eventually sold and torn down.

Chapter 10

# TAKING THE GOSPEL TO THE WORLD

Out in the hedges and highways of life,
Many are weary and sad,
Taking the sunshine where darkness is rife,
Making the sorrowing glad—
Make me a blessing.

During the lifetime of B. R. Lakin the world saw many miraculous and astounding changes. In the year of his birth the world saw two unique inventions: the disposable razor blade and the ice cream cone. Eventually modernization even reached the mountain men of West Virginia and Lakin's transportation changed from mules and buggies to automobiles and jet airplanes. His meeting places changed from tents to tabernacles. But one thing never changed—in this land or around the world his one simple message was: "Man is a sinner; Christ a Saviour. There is a heaven to gain and a hell to shun. Life is short and eternity is long. Prepare to meet your God."

It was obvious that the gift of B. R. Lakin was exhortation through preaching. Whether it was to a small crowd of mountain people or to the polished urbanites of Detroit, Lakin loved to preach about Jesus. He had a simple philosophy: "My father used to tell me on the farm, always put the fodder down low in the rack for the calves to get to it. I've heard a lot of preachers preach and I felt like they put it so high that only ecclesiastical giraffes could ever get to it. Gypsy Smith said his father said 'Never use more than two syllable words that will explain your meaning.' So I never used any of these 16-cylinder, triple jointed words. You wouldn't understand them if I did. I could manufacture a few—like when my boy was a little fellow, if he'd come in one day and pulled a dead rat out of his pocket—he might have done it—and I would say to him, 'William, my olfactory organs tell me that the rodent that you now have in your possession has through some chemical compound or other arrived at a high state of putrefaction. I think it would be the height of wisdom to convey same hence.' Why he'd be nonplussed! But if I said, 'Hey kid, that's rotten!', he'd grab his nose and scram."

Once an old woman told Dr. Lakin that she liked to hear him preach because he was "such a simple preacher." Lakin laughed, "I don't know whether she meant I was a simpleton or I made things plain." Those who knew him know that he made things plain—often to the point of bluntness.

Once a man was driving him to Detroit through a blizzard. Dr. Lakin told the man that he was a Baptist preacher, and the man was quick to reply, "Well, I'm an atheist. I don't believe there is a God."

Dr. Lakin didn't pause for a moment. "Sir, I saw your name in the Bible."

"You never saw my name!"

"Oh yes, I did." Dr. Lakin took a little testament and read, " 'For the fool has said in his heart, there is no God.' Mr. Fool, I'm glad to know you."

Not many people could get away with such brashness, but there was a simplicity about Dr. Lakin which disallowed malice. He was simply honest.

When he was a young preacher in Ceredo, West Virginia, several older preachers were present in his Sunday afternoon meeting. After his message, one of them approached him.

"Young man, that was a marvellous message. If you would leave certain things off, you would be a great preacher."

"How many do you preach to?" retorted Lakin.

"Oh, I have a membership of about 600" replied the pastor.

"No, I didn't ask you that. How many do you preach to?"

The pastor faltered for a moment. "Oh, I would say about 60."

Lakin said, "I preach to a full house every Sunday

morning. If I left certain things off, I would be as no 'count for the Lord as you are."

The houses continued to be full wherever Dr. Lakin preached. As he pastored the Cadle Tabernacle, he spent nearly every night preaching somewhere across the

The Lakins in Hawaii, where he was holding revival meetings.

nation. Buford Cadle and Dr. Lakin bought a Bonanza— an airplane which the tabernacle purchased new from the factory for just over $8,000.

Buford Cadle flew Dr. Lakin out to his meetings so that he could make those one-night services. In those days, preachers with private planes were uncommon, but Dr. Lakin's 50,000-mile per year schedule demanded fast transportation.

As many as four and five thousand people gathered in large auditoriums to hear the country preacher. The Cincinnati Music Hall was crammed with six thousand

One of the crowds which eagerly came to hear B. R. Lakin. Dr. Lakin and Mrs. Lakin are in the center front.

people every night for a week long crusade. But whether it was on ball fields, civic auditoriums, or in high school gymnasiums, the crowds flocked to hear Dr. B. R. Lakin. It was not uncommon for as many as 15,000 people to pack a fairground to hear the country preacher, and Lakin once addressed a crowd of 25,000.

The consuming desire of Lakin's life was to see revival break out across this nation. He asked God to let him see a revival, but he knew revival does not come without paying a price. He paid the price daily for 66 years. "What will it take for America to return to God?" he often asked. "I remember the recession after World War I. Eleven million people stood in breadlines. And yet America did not return to God. Then there was a period of prosperity. Everything we touched turned to gold—and still we did not acknowledge God. Now I believe the vials of God's wrath are fast filling up, and He will pour them out upon this nation and others in a rapidity that will startle. I believe the only thing that will stay the hand of judgment is a return to God and an old-fashioned, genuine, Holy Ghost, limb-straightening, heaven-opening, Devil-driving revival."

During his preaching career he was honored in a

multitude of ways: he once opened the Tri-State Fair, held in Huntington, West Virginia, and was escorted from the airport to the fairgrounds by a motorcycle brigade. He was commissioned as a Kentucky Colonel by Governor John R. Brown. When he arrived in Richlands, Virginia, to hold a series of meetings, the entire town welcomed him with a parade and a brass band. When the bridge which linked Louisa, Kentucky, and Fort Gay, West Virginia, was freed from the toll which paid for its construction, Dr. Lakin shared in the ceremonies with two state governors.

The Lakin Family was invited back to Fort Gay, West Virginia, for homecoming.

He was often called the "Prince of Preachers." When he entered full time evangelism in 1952, he continued to stay very busy while Mrs. Lakin made their home comfortable.

The Lakins chose to make their home base in Titusville, Florida because of the warm climate and pleasant surroundings. Along with the towns of Cocoa, Cocoa Beach, and Merritt Island, Titusville is a part of Florida's "Space Coast". These towns are literally across the river from Cape Canaveral and the Lakins could stand in their front yard and see the rocket launches. Mrs. Lakin would always chuckle when the dishes in the cabinets rattled from the intense sound of the rocket engines. Life was good and progress was exciting.

Bill and Cathy were doing well in Florida and Ronnie grew to be an adorable, bright boy who quickly became the apple of his grandpop's eye.

A big crowd from a tiny town turned out to hear the preacher.

One hot July, the Lakins were invited back to Fort Gay for the small town's homecoming. As the Lakins drove onto the main street they saw the huge banner which had been strung from two telephone poles: "Mass Meeting 11 a.m. and 2:30 p.m. Welcome Home Dr. B. R. Lakin."

The Lakin Family at the homecoming: Dr. and Mrs. Lakin; Bill and his wife, Cathy; and Ronnie, Dr. Lakin's grandson.

A small wooden platform had been built for Dr. Lakin and nearly every folding chair in town had been set out on the church lawn. At 2:30 on that hot afternoon, as the women fanned themselves and the electric fans on the platform tried vainly to circulate the air, Dr. Lakin stood to address his friends and relatives. The small children sat spellbound as he spoke, and the people of the town nudged each other and whispered emphatically, "He sure can preach."

"To whom is the Gospel an offense?" roared Dr. Lakin. "You tell that woman tonight that sparkles and scintillates with diamonds and rustles with silks and satins, moral and upright, clean in deportment; tell her tonight that she needs a Saviour. She needs to be born again the same as the harlot in the slums. Tell that cultured, refined, respectable gentleman tonight, tell that professional or businessman tonight that he needs a Saviour, that he needs to be born again the same as the drunken bum on the street of forgotten men. That's where the Gospel becomes an offense. I'm telling you tonight, that men and women everywhere need a Saviour, regardless of the degree of their sin."

Dr. Lakin was loved by everyone. A plaque which hangs in his office reads "To Dr. B. R. Lakin: Happy Father's Day to the spiritual father of thousands with gratitude for 56 years of 'plowing, planting, and watering.' "

While pastoring, Dr. Lakin continued his evangelistic work. This is Akron Baptist Temple, one of Dr. Lakin's favorite places.

Lakin stopped a moment and chuckled. "Oh, I love to preach, amen. If people wouldn't hire me to preach, I'd hire 'em to let me. When I get to heaven, I'm going to take a few of the angels over in the corner and preach to them awhile 'cause I know something they don't know—the joy of Christ's salvation."

After the sermon, the church provided a good old-fashioned dinner on the grounds, and Bill, Cathy, Ronnie, and the Lakins had a great time sharing and fellowshipping with their friends. When it was all over, the people of Fort Gay went home, proud that a son of their town had become such a fine preacher—and a fine man.

# Chapter 11

# ABIDING JOY

**A merry heart doeth good like a medicine**
*—Proverbs 17:22*

One preacher said of Lakin, "He was the funniest man I ever met. His timing—I think he could have supplanted Bob Hope anytime. I think that if he had gone the route of Hollywood instead of the route of the Gospel ministry, he would have been a household name around the world. His timing and humor were a God-given ability. You can't learn that in school."

Lakin was funny in and out of the pulpit. One of his funniest sermon illustrations was about evolution: "My niece came home from college one day and said to me, 'Uncle, the professor at school said that Jesus couldn't have been born of a human mother without a human father. He said that was a biological impossibility.'"

"And I said, 'Well, ring a ding ling. You tell the little possum-headed professor that I said that the first man that ever got in this world got here without either father or mother. And if the first man got here without father or mother, if God wanted to send His Son born of a human mother without a human father, He could and did do it. Amen?"

"The next day she came back to explain how the first germ came from another planet."

"Well, the first germ got here without father or mother. Life has never been generated from dead matter. Where did the first germ come from?"

"She said, 'It came from another planet on a meteor.' "

"I said, 'Honey, don't you know a meteor is a blazing ball of fire? How could a live germ live in that?"

"She said, 'The theory of evolution is the only sane explanation.' "

"That's the most insane thing I have ever heard. To be an evolutionist, all you got to do is to stultify your brain and throw your reason out of gear, that's all. Let me tell you something—if you tell me that's a scientific evolution theory to creation, that a way back yonder somewhere, somehow, nobody knows when, how, where, or why, nothing got in nothing and something formed out of nothing. A germ got in the water somehow. Then the water developed it into a tadpole and the tadpole swam too near the bank one day and got stuck in the mud and dried there. Wriggling around in the mud, he formed warts on his belly that later became legs. After he developed legs, he became a land animal and climbing through the trees one day, his foot slipped and he fell—the jar broke off his tail. He hit the ground, walked across the street, bought him a suit of clothes, began teaching in the university and said, 'Thank God, I'm a man at last.' "

When asked "Where did Cain get his wife?", Dr. Lakin always replied, "From his mother-in-law, the same place I got mine."

Lakin inserted his country humor into nearly every sermon. While discussing whether the saints would have wings in heaven, he said, "Once a lady said to me, 'When I die, what puzzles me is how I will get my robe on over my wings.' I told her, 'What puzzles me is how you'll get your hat on over your horns.' "

"And then I hear them sing, 'I want to be an angel and with the angels stand.' It was a great disappointment to some when they found out they would never be angel. A fellow said he married one—she's always up in the air, harping on something."

"You know every preacher ought to be reared in the country, amen? I mean an old-fashioned coon-hunting, possum-hunting preacher. Now you talk about possum hunting, these city slickers don't know anything about that. If you go down in my country, back in the head of the holler, they'll know what you mean. You ever go possum hunting?"

"An old boy got sick, way back there in the head of the holler; he never had seen an electric light. They had to take him by wagon to the hospital in Huntington. They reached the top of the ridge which overlooks Huntington at about midnight. That old boy raised up and saw all the lights in the valley and said, 'Good Lord, the whole world has gone possum hunting, ain't they?'"

Yes, Lakin loved life. In the middle of a hard driving sermon on the pleasures of sin, he interrupted his tirade against pleasure-seeking to say, "What's wrong with pleasure seeking? Do I believe in pleasure seeking? Yes. You never looked a fellow between two big brown eyes that's getting more fun out of living than I am."

When looking out over his congregation, Lakin would often remark, "I like to see you smile when you come to church. I like to read in the Bible 'for the joy of the Lord is your strength,' not your gloominess. I don't think the Lord ever intended for us to come to church with a tombstone under one arm and a coffin under the other, looking like the advance agent for an undertaker. So many Christians are like the lady who said, 'I always feel bad when I feel good 'cause I know I'm going to feel worse.'"

"But I believe Christians ought to be sweet. We ought to be so sweet that if a fellow hits you on the shoulder he'll get honey on his hand and wander down the street licking it off and wondering how he can get saved."

Dr. Lakin admitted, "Some people say I'm a nut. That may be so, but at least I'm screwed onto the right bolt, amen? When the Lord made me, He smiled and threw the pattern away—He never fixed it. There's only one of me."

A fellow once criticized Dr. Lakin's preaching, "I don't get anything to take home with me after hearing you preach."

Dr. Lakin retorted, "That's because you didn't bring anything to get it in, that's what's the matter. I'm able to furnish the point, but I can't furnish the intelligence to see it with."

There wasn't much Lakin couldn't get away with. Although he was very generous and freely supported other ministries, he was once upset to find that someone had their fingers in his offering plate. The church had taken a love offering of $1200.00 on the first night of his meeting, and the deacons hated to part with the money. Unknown to them, while they sat in one room inventing expenses to deduct from the love offering, Lakin was praying in the next room and overheard every word.

The next night of the meeting Lakin took his briefcase with him onto the platform. After the ushers took the offering, Lakin opened the briefcase and held it up. "You boys just bring that offering here," he directed. "Put it here in my briefcast. You can trust me with my own money."

Dr. Lakin loved to eat dinner in the homes of his friends. He preferred puttering around in someone's kitchen to sitting in fancy restaurants. Once he was invited to supper at Bill Pennell's house and Lakin especially requested chili. As Betty Pennell was putting ingredients into a big pot on the stove, Lakin came in and said, "Now you make it plenty hot."

"Do you want it **spice** hot or **fire** hot?" she asked.

Lakin didn't hesitate. "I want it hell hot."

He had a way with words and a mind filled with fun. Young and old alike flocked to the side of the fun-loving preacher. Often he'd pull into a town at four a.m., check into a motel, and call a pastor friend of his to ask, "Hey preacher—you got anything to eat?"

You never knew what to expect from Lakin. On one of his fourteen trips to the Holy Land he stood outside of Beersheba eating one of the large oranges which are grown there. A fellow traveler asked him, "Dr. Lakin, you're a Bible scholar. The Bible says there are 12 fruits on the Tree of Life in Heaven. Do you know what those fruits will be?"

Lakin took a moment to wipe the juice from his mouth. "Can't say for sure, but one of them's tuitti fruiti."

Lakin's jovial spirit and optimistic attitude made him a very pleasant person to be around. He made everyone comfortable in his presence. But the warmth which came from his heart was primarily a tool to introduce people to the heart of God.

He said, "If you want to know what God looks like, what His power is, look at the flowers—you see His wisdom. Look at the stars—you see His glory. Look at the ocean—you see his power. But look at Calvary and you see His heart. If you want to know Him, come to Calvary. When you see Jesus dying on that cross you see the heart of God."

# Chapter 12

# THE MAN WITH A BROKEN HEART

**The bustle in a house**
**The morning after death**
**Is solemnest of industries**
**Enacted upon earth,—**

**The sweeping up the heart,**
**And putting love away**
**We shall not want to use again**
**Until eternity.** —*Emily Dickinson*

On March 27, 1955, Dr. Lakin was preaching in Akron, Ohio, one of his favorite places. The pastor of the host church, Dr. Carl Burnham, had been saved under Dr. Lakin's ministry and the meetings had been very successful.

Back at home in Florida, Mrs. Lakin and Bill were busy. Bill decided to drive over to Merritt Island with a friend to check on some construction, but while they were driving, Bill suddenly became silent and the car swerved out of control. When the car finally came to a stop, Bill was dead.

At first it was supposed that Bill had broken his neck in the collision, but one examining doctor disagreed and blamed it on Bill's poor heart. The other man in the car was not injured at all; Bill only had one small bruise on his cheek.

Mrs. Lakin received the news and sat numbly. In no time at all, the pastor of the church the Lakins attended was at her home. "I'll call Dr. Lakin," he volunteered.

"Well, he'll have to know it," she said, "But I'll have two to bury."

It was one a.m. when Dr. Lakin received a call from his pastor in Florida. "Dr. Lakin," he began, "Something terrible happened here. Bill had a wreck, and it's fatal." Dr. Lakin sat stiffly, unable to comprehend. His wife's voice came over the line. "Honey," she said, "I'll bring his body and meet you in West Virginia."

As soon as the word spread through Akron, several preachers rushed to offer aid. As he faced them in his motel room, he said, "Well, I'll have to go on. That's it." Dr. Lakin refused all offers of assistance and drove alone from Ohio to his home in West Virginia. As he drove, he relived the days from Bill's life, happy days of love and

The Lakins' son, Bill, while a student at Greenbrier Military Academy.

togetherness. He had been so proud of his son! And now, at age 31, Bill's life was over. There would be no son to take up the mantle of his ministry.

When Mrs. Lakin arrived at their log home in Fort Gay, she met her husband on the stairs. "How can we go on?" she began, "I'll never be reconciled."

Dr. Lakin replied, "Oh, yes, we must and can. For 35 years I've told people, 'God's grace is sufficient.' If it isn't sufficient for you and me now, I've not been honest in preaching to others."

Dr. Lakin said, "People ask me now, 'Dr. Lakin, have you ever asked God why?' No. Because some day, up in heaven, He'll make it plain. And until then I'll watch and wait."

Dr. and Mrs. Lakin buried Bill under an oak tree in their hillside family cemetery in West Virginia. One morning, as they walked silently up the hill to stand beside the grave, Dr. Lakin felt the Spirit of Christ speaking to him: "I know how you feel. I had a little family over in Bethany I used to love and visit—Martha and Mary and Lazarus. But one day Lazarus got sick, and before I could get there he died and was put in the tomb.

Bill Lakin while serving on the *U. S. Stevens* during World War II.

I went over there and stood and wept. I am the resurrection and the life. He that liveth and believeth in me, though he were dead, yet shall he live."

Dr. Lakin believed that a new power comes from crushing experiences, that a rose must be bruised before you get perfume from it. Dr. Lakin said, "From the night I received the message that Bill was in an automobile accident and it was fatal—from that hour until this— I've had a broken and crushed heart. I thank God for all of it." Sorrow made the Lakins draw closer to Jesus. With great anticipation B. R. looked toward the day he would be with Bill forever.

"I preached for Dr. Billington not long after that; we had four thousand people that night. I preached on

Samson. Samson's hair was cut off, but the root of the matter was still there. And that which was in eventually began to come out. If you get your hair cut off, if it's your own hair, you can expect it to grow. If it's just a religious wig, it won't grow.''

"And the Bible says that Samson could feel that old power surge once more. And unknown and unnoticed by them, his hair began to grow again. And he said to the little boy, 'Hey, kid, lead me out there.' And he went out and leaned upon those pillars. And he said, 'Lord, I'm not fit to be heard, but hear me one more time.' And he pulled the pillars down and killed more in his death than he had in his life.''

"And don't you fellows go out and sing 'The bird with the broken pinion never soared so high again.' I believe a man can have these things come upon him and come back with renewed power. Samson said, 'Lord, I know I'm not fit to be heard, but I'd rather die than live among these Philistines.' Would you rather die than live outside the will of God?''

That night, over 100 people were saved in Dr. Billington's church. Dr. Billington caught Dr. Lakin after the service and said, "Bill killed more in his death than he ever did in his life.''

"What do you mean?'' asked Dr. Lakin.

"Because you're preaching with a different power—different than I've ever heard you.''

In later years, Dr. Lakin came to believe "You'll never be what you ought to be until your heart's been broken.''

Dr. Lakin always demonstrated the love of God as he preached to the bereaved. He said, "You can trust God, my friend. My dad and mother pillowed their heads upon that hope and passed peacefully into another world. The man who denies it stands without any hope in this world and in the world to come. He has no hope of meeting with his loved ones who have gone or who may go. Buried out yonder lies my boy on a little hillside in West Virginia, in a grave, waiting for the resurrection. One day I believe he will come forth from the grave and I'll see him again. God hangs a rainbow of hope around the shimmering shoulders of the storm of my bereavement. He is that hope and without Him there is no hope of pardon in the eternal world. Why do I believe there is a God, my friend?

Because only He makes any sense out of this old world. Only He brings meaning to living, the hope of pardon, and a place in heaven."

Dr. Lakin was able to preach when he was sick, tired, and brokenhearted because he shared the "fellowship of His sufferings." He believed, "You'll never see a rainbow except you see it through the raindrops; neither will you see a glorified life except you see it through the teardrops of Calvary."

# Chapter 13

# LABORING THROUGH PHYSICAL PAIN

**Other sheep are there to gather,**
**Wand'ring far o'er hill and plain.**
**Who will guide them back to shelter?**
**Hark! I hear Him call my name.**
**Hark! I hear Him call my name,**
**Not to fortune or to fame;**
**But to gather in the lost ones:**
**Hark! I hear Him call my name.**
*—S. N. Fitkin*

Although B. R. Lakin was a husky man, strengthened by a childhood of farm work and a busy schedule, he was afflicted by a heart condition. It was this weakness which often plagued him late in life, and it nearly ended his promising preaching when he was still a young man.

Early in his ministry, he was preaching in Ashland, Kentucky, when he was suddenly taken with a mysterious ailment. He was rushed to the hospital and the doctors on duty in the emergency room quickly examined him and found no heartbeat. As his wife and three-year old son stood nearby, the doctors declared Lakin dead, the newspapers were called, and his obituary was written to appear the next day.

But, by some miracle of God, B. R. Lakin lived and thrived. But in the last few years of his life, he became quite ill with diabetes, a weakened heart, and terrible circulation. His doctors almost amputated his leg once, and he began to carry a cane as he preached. When he learned that he had diabetes, he said, "I asked the Lord to make me sweet and He overdid it."

While at the Cadle Tabernacle, Dr. Lakin was diagnosed as having spinal arthritis. An x-ray showed that his spine was beginning to crumble. He wore a back brace and often had to lean on the pulpit as he preached to take the pressure off his back. He was in tremendous pain, but he kept preaching.

But, during a short vacation at their West Virginia cabin, a preacher from a little Wesleyan-Methodist church visited the Lakins. "You know," he remarked to Mrs. Lakin, "I believe God would heal him."

Dr. Lakin also preached in tents. After leaving Cadle Tabernacle, the Lakins moved to Titusville, Florida, and went into evangelistic work full time.

The "Prince of Preachers" continued to spread the Gospel despite failing health. He often said, "No matter what may be the means or method that hour comes to me, if you read or hear on the news that I have died, don't you believe it. That day will be Graduation Day, and I will have just begun to live. I will merely have changed my base of operation. I won't be dead; I'll just have moved out for repairs."

Mrs. Lakin and the visiting preacher each knelt by the side of Dr. Lakin's bed and prayed that he would be healed. "Something happened," Dr. Lakin said, "because I don't wear a brace anymore, amen? I don't believe in divine healers, but I certainly do believe in divine healing."

He continued to preach. When other preachers would have called it quits and settled down to rest, Dr. Lakin continued his "bragging on Jesus." He did not know the meaning of retirement. At 76 years of age he was holding meetings every night. He had a deep conviction that God called him to preach for as long as he had strength. Although his physical problems increased with his age, Dr. Lakin maintained a full schedule until 1982.

He often said, "No matter what may be the means or method that hour comes to me, if you read or hear on the news that I have died, don't you believe it. That day will be Graduation Day, and I will have just begun to live. I will merely have changed my base of operation. I won't be dead; I'll just have moved out for repairs."

Dr. Lakin traveled in a van until poor circulation in his legs made it impossible to tolerate hours of riding. But he didn't quit; he cried out to the Lord, "God, if I'm going to go on, I've got to do something."

In 1972, the pastors and churches of the Baptist Bible Fellowship presented Dr. Lakin with a comfortable Winnebago for his travels. This enabled him to stretch out and ease the numbness in his legs and also provided a way for Mrs. Lakin to travel with him. More often, however, Ronnie Lakin drove for his grandfather.

But during the last few years of his life, driving and riding was practically impossible. Dr. Lakin had to be flown to most of his meetings. Despite his failing health, he would get up in the morning and drive off to the airport to preach even when his wife doubted that he had the strength to stand in the pulpit. Ronnie once asked him, "Poppop, why do you keep going day and night this way?"

Dr. Lakin responded, "Son, you wouldn't understand. Poppop believes this Bible is the word of God. He believes there is a hell and he believes that men die without Jesus Christ and spend eternity in Hell. When I'm gone, I don't care whether you build a shaft of marble or a monument of granite, it doesn't matter. But when you stand beside my grave, I want you to say, 'My poppop never left me any fortune. He never left me any riches, but he left behind a life that was big and rich and ripe, and blessed humanity. A quarter of a million souls have taken his hand and been pointed toward Jesus.' "

Dr. Lakin once heard the story of Catherine Mumford Booth, the co-founder of the Salvation Army. When "Grandmother Booth" died in 1890, her body lay in state in London. The city organized special trains to carry

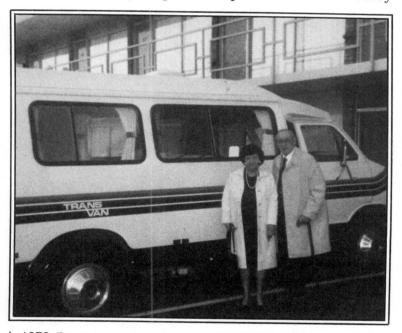

In 1972, the pastors and churches of the Baptist Bible Fellowship presented Dr. Lakin with a comfortable Winnebago for his travels. This photo shows Dr. and Mrs. Lakin later with a van, provided by a friend in California.

mourners to view her casket. The lines stretched for blocks, and policemen were employed to keep the crowds moving. One woman lifted her small daughter up and the policeman urged her to hurry along. "But officer," the woman protested, "I was a woman of the street and this woman led me to Christ. I wanted my daughter to see her." Later a man stopped by the side of the casket. With

As usual when he traveled, Violet was by his side.

tears cutting through the grime on his workman's face, he told the policeman, "I was a drunken bum until this lady led me to Christ." The people filed by the casket until Grandmother Booth's shroud was as wet with tears as if it had been dipped in water.

When Dr. Lakin heard this story, he turned to his companions and said, "I'd rather be that woman and wear that old tear-stained shroud at the coronation of my Lord

For many years, Dr. Lakin's grandson, Ronnie, accompanied him on his travels.

than to be a society woman that sparkles with diamonds and lives a wasted life and dies and is soon forgotten."

Everything was worth the effort expended if it resulted in the spreading of the Gospel, Dr. Lakin believed. He knew about that bitter cup of pain. "I went to see a little old lady one day. She was sitting in a wheelchair with her hands twisted and her little feet were twisted, too. She reached up her little hand and said, 'Dr. Lakin, nobody in this world knows what I suffer.' I replied, 'Nobody in this world, but there's one in heaven who knows.' "

Mrs. Lakin knew that her husband's failing health was no match for his busy schedule. But she also knew his restless personality. He felt that he had much to do and little time in which to do it. After Bill Lakin died, Mrs. Lakin wanted to keep busy so she became a realtor. She was the first successful female realtor in the area, but as Dr. Lakin's health became poor, she stopped working and began to travel by her husband's side.

Once as Dr. Lakin was preparing to leave on a four-week preaching trip he was too weak to make it down the stairs of their home without help. As Mrs. Lakin held

Ronnie Lakin "on the road" with his grandfather. One night Dr. Lakin and Ronnie were driving during the early morning hours. Ronnie turned to Dr. Lakin and asked, "Poppop, why do you keep going like this day after day, night after night?" Dr. Lakin replied, "It would be hard for you to understand. But when I die and you stand beside my grave, I will not care about a granite stone or a monument of marble; I would like you and others to be able to say, 'Dr. Lakin never left a fortune, but he left behind a life that was big and rich and ripe, and blessed humanity. A quarter of a million souls have taken his hand and been pointed toward Jesus.'"

his arm she asked, "Why don't you just call these people and tell them you can't come?"

Lakin responded quickly, "Listen here, sister. The old Devil is not going to defeat me. I'll claim the blood against him and I'll trust Him—'As my days are, so shall my strength be.' "

Whenever he underwent physical difficulty, Dr. Lakin thought about the physical difficulties of Jesus. "He had a body just like ours that got tired and had to sit on a well curb to rest and refresh itself. He had to go to sleep on a boat. They took that body of infirmities, just like ours, and nailed it on a cross. Round and round the cycle of suffering he went until, with a parched throat and swollen lips he cried, 'My God, my God, why has thou forsaken me?' That's the only time He ever called the father 'God'. God is not the father of the unsaved. So when He who knew no sin became sin for us, God thrust Him out, pulled the curtain of darkness between Himself and His Son, and let Him feel what it was to be left alone, the first time He'd been left alone since the morning stars sang together. He then dropped His chin upon His pulseless chest and said, 'It is finished.' He suffered our pain. He reached over the battlements of Heaven and plucked the thorn of suffering from the pillow of every sufferer in this world."

The years of travel and endless work were hard on Dr. Lakin, but he never forgot his roots. He recently went back to Fort Gay to visit his nephew, he stopped by the little creek where he was baptized. "I knelt there and let the water run through my fingers," he once said, "and then I said, 'Lord, a lot of water's gone over these rocks in the last sixty years.' "

He went on up to the little church where a crowd of sixty-eight people had gathered. The old church had burned, and a new brick building had been erected fifty yards from the previous site. Lakin and his nephew walked across the church yard and Lakin said, "Jim—about here is where the old church was, wasn't it?" Jim agreed. Lakin then walked a few steps further and murmured, "I think it was about here where, on that night, I knelt at the pine mourner's bench and met Jesus. The deep, settled peace that came into my soul that night has withstood the crush of woes and the test of time."

Chapter 14

# THE WORK CONTINUES

**Great works are performed not by strength but by perseverance.** —*Samuel Johnson*

After fifteen years in Titusville, Florida, Dr. Lakin felt impressed by the Lord to move back to the mountains. In 1967, he and Mrs. Lakin moved back to their log home in Fort Gay and Dr. Lakin began another radio broadcast: "The Voice of the Appalachians." A chain of radio stations throughout the mountain counties of the Carolinas, Tennessee, Virginia, and West Virginia broadcast the program.

After six years in the mountains, Lakin asked Dr. Louis Arnold to assume his responsibilities with the radio program and the Lakins made plans to move back to Florida. B. R. was thinking of retiring.

"Mrs. Lakin and I discussed it, and we decided that I'd go down to Huntington and finish some radio tapes and then we'd retire. I was in the inner office making a tape, and she was in the outer office doing some work. I was preaching and yelling like I had 100 people in there, and she was out there listening to me. I was preaching on the verse, 'Occupy until I come!' and I had preached myself under conviction. When I came out, she said, 'Anybody that can preach like that has got no business retiring.' I said, 'You want me to work myself to death, don't you?' She said, 'No, but they need your message.' "

Dr. Lakin once again entered full time evangelism, and found that his schedule was booked eighteen months in advance. When asked how he promoted himself, Dr. Lakin said, "Not one thing have I ever done to promote myself. I just started preaching with all my might, riding a mule with a pair of saddlebags to a little country church. God has led me every step of the way and taken care of all the promotion."

The Lakins spent many years together in Christian service. They co-labored for the cause of Christ without weighing the cost.

The telephone and mail brought five requests for a meeting every day, yet Dr. Lakin never asked for one single meeting. He was traveling over 50,000 miles a year, speaking to approximately 4,000 people each week.

Why did he travel so much and so often? Because he felt a consuming desire to take the Gospel to the people. "Sometimes I think some of our big churches are simply like the disciples were on the Mount of Transfiguration.

On the road
with Dr. Lakin
and his tent
ministry.

They say 'Here is a good place to be, so let's remain.' Some of our big churches have brought in mahogany pews, stained glass windows, brilliant preachers, and well-trained choirs. They say 'Now here we are, come and find us' but the lost haven't found them. Nowhere did God command the unsaved man to go and find the church, but He told the church to go out after the unsaved."

He lived up to the promise he made when he knelt at the little pine mourner's bench on that long-ago night in West Virginia: "Lord, if you'll save me, you'll never hear the last of it."

Pastor Bill Pennell is one of those who invited Lakin to speak in his church. He believes that Dr. Lakin has had a profound influence on his life. "I sat at Dr. Lakin's feet and listened to him for hours. I drove many mailes to hear him preach. I am a fundamental independent Baptist preacher today because of his influence. I believe Dr. Lakin was the greatest preacher alive in his day. I have seen him on his knees in a motel room beseeching God with heart-rendering prayers full of power and love for souls. I have seen him with tears streaming down his face. He showed me what it means to live a life that is totally surrendered to God."

In April, 1978, Dr. Lakin held meetings in the church pastored by Dr. Roy Thompson. That week, 147 people were saved. Dr. Thompson said it was the best revival they have ever had—on Sunday they could not get all the people inside the auditorium. "Dr. Lakin is my daddy in the faith. As a 19-year-old alcoholic, I was saved under Dr. Lakin's ministry. When my family and I first started our church in an empty tavern, Dr. Lakin came. He was never too big to hold meetings in small churches. Today we are averaging over 2,000."

Once a young preacher asked Dr. Lakin if he held meetings in small churches. "No," Lakin replied.

The young preacher shrugged and said, "Well, I just thought I'd ask."

Dr. Lakin continued, "There are no small churches. Nothing is small if God is in it."

Dr. H. Frank Collins was called into the ministry under Dr. Lakin's ministry. "Dr. Lakin was very precious to me. He was very influential in my early ministry. He counseled with me and advised me many long hours. I have seen more love in his ministry than in the ministry of any other man living."

J. Randall Smith lives in Mansfield, Ohio. He first heard Dr. Lakin preaching on the radio from Cadle Tabernacle. As a nine-year-old boy, when Randy Smith heard Dr. Lakin say that Cadle Tabernacle had 19 doors, Randy thought it had to be the biggest church in the world. Most churches got by with only two.

Randy's grandfather had been a jailer in Fort Gay, West Virginia, and he'd often tell his grandson stories about the feuding Hatfields and McCoys. But just as often, he'd tell stories about the mighty preacher that came from those parts—B. R. Lakin. Randy couldn't wait to meet him.

Randy drove 100 miles to hear Dr. Lakin preach in person. When he finally stood to shake the hand of the man he had admired for so many years, he found a pair of kindly eyes twinkling back at him. All he had to do was mention Fort Gay, and Randy found a friend for life.

A few years later, Dr. Lakin preached in Mansfield, and Randy wanted to take his hero out for dinner. "No," said Lakin, "I want a good Fort Gay dinner like down home. Can your wife fix soup beans, corn bread, fried potatoes, and lettuce with hot bacon drippings poured over the top? And I want a real big onion; I don't want any little onions."

Randy enjoyed his Fort Gay lunch with Dr. Lakin and now the plate and silverware Dr. Lakin ate from are framed and hanging in Randy Smith's home. "I will always remember how down home he was," Randy said. "Even though he was well known all over, he was a simple man who made everyone feel at ease to talk to him. Even his messages were simple so everyone could understand the truth of God."

# Chapter 15

# AN OPINION
# ON EVERYTHING

**Opinion in good men is but knowledge in the making.**
*—John Milton*

**On World Politics:**
"You will remember when Mr. Kosygin came to this country and met with President Johnson up in New Jersey. I said that the Red Star of Russia and the Lone Star of Texas had a meeting about the Star of David but said very little about the Star of Bethlehem. At that time, Mr. Kosygin said, 'Russia is always for peace.' Oh, they believe in peace, the Communists do. They believe in a piece of this and a piece of that. Well, Mr. Kosygin said that Israel was going to have to give back some of their land to the Arabs. And I said, 'Look who's talking! Why doesn't he give back Czechoslovakia, Rumania, Bulgaria, Cuba—why doesn't he give that back? I've got news for him—Israel is not only going to keep their present land, they're going to get more. They have a title deed to the land in the book of Genesis.' "

**On World Economics:**
"Every nation in the world is bankrupt. They've taxed everything they can tax except the wind you breathe, and I'm expecting them to put a meter on my windpipe most any day."

**On World History:**
"I've studied the rise and fall of the Old Roman Empire.

I found the Roman Empire fell because of three things. First, they rotted morally. Second, they became sports crazy. Third, they were overtaxed. The situation became unbearable."

"Now, are we following the same pattern? Are we rotten morally? With dope and immorality, sex—the whole business of immorality and godlessness beyond natural affection. Are we sports crazy? Just like the Romans, we're building coliseums that can seat thousands of people, all jammed in for one thing. Overtaxation—that's where we are."

## On the World Council of Churches:

"I anticipate that eventually apostate Protestantism and apostate Catholicism will join hands under the name of Universal Brotherhood. A good Catholic friend of mine once said, 'Dr. Lakin, I don't understand. I was taught as a child that it was wrong to eat meat on Friday. Now they're saying it's alright. What's happened?' I replied, 'Do you want me to tell you what happened? They are watering down to take these weak-kneed protestants in. And that's the reason I'm against the ecumenical movement. That's why I'm against the World Council of Churches. I'm not going to aid and assist in the creation of the Great Harlot, I'm not going to do it. Nowhere in the Bible did God say, Come together. He said, Come out from among them and be ye separate.' "

## On the Inerrancy of Scripture:

"A little two-by-squirt said to me not long ago, 'Do you believe the Bible contains the Word of God?' and I said, 'No, I believe it is the Word of God.' From the first word of Genesis to the last word in the book of the Revelation, it is the verbally-inspired, inerrantly accurate, God-breathed Word of God."

## On Science:

"The Bible is a thousand years ahead of science. I remember when the astronauts first went up, I listened to a news reporter state, 'Now we can prove that the earth is round.' Well, Isaiah said that before he ever said it."

"When the astronomers looked toward the north and

saw a space that had no stars in it, they thought they had discovered something. But the Bible said, 'He stretches out the North over the empty spaces and hangeth the earth upon nothing.'"

"How long did it take us to discover germs? They knew about it in the Bible. Scripture commands, 'And this shall be the law of the leper. He shall go down the street with a cloth on his upper lip and shall cry, Unclean, unclean.'"

**On Israel:**

"The story of the Jews is a bigger miracle than Jonah and the big fish. God commissioned Jonah to Nineveh, and he was disobedient. God commissioned Israel to show forth His glory thoughout the nations of the earth, and they were disobedient. Jonah boarded a ship and started away to Joppa, running away from God. Israel was disobedient and ran away from God. God didn't let Jonah go, He pursued him with storms. And God pursued Israel with storms, and said, 'Cursed shall be thy basket and thy store.' And Jonah cried unto the Lord as the waves flowed over him. And in the day of Jacob's trouble, Israel will cry unto the Lord. And God caused the whale to spit Jonah up and God will cause the nations of this earth to give back the Jews. As for three days and three nights Jonah was preserved in the belly of the fish, so will Israel be preserved in the bowels of other nations."

**On Prayer:**

"I wonder if you ever went to an automat—that's a restaurant that looks like a post office. You go in and you don't see any cook, any waiter, or any waitress. You drop in a quarter, out comes some pie and coffee, you drop in fifteen cents and out comes something else."

"I went to New York one day, and, being a country boy, I tried it out. I went in, dropped in the money, and out it came. But I wasn't a big enough fool to believe that there wasn't somebody back there passing that stuff out."

"For fifty-three years I've walked up to the open window of Heaven and I've had stuff passed out to me just as real as mashed potatoes and gravy. And that's the reason I know there is a God—He answers prayer."

## On Cults:

"A fella once said to me, 'These cults and false religions have taken almost all the people I have.' I replied, 'That's your fault. If you had founded them in the Word, they wouldn't have run.'"

"A traveling man rode up to the farmer's door and said, 'Your hogs have gone crazy. I watched them a while ago, and they ran squealing across the field to the other side and then they turned around and came squealing around back to this side.' The old farmer said, 'No, they're not crazy, but last winter I lost my voice and I couldn't call my hogs except by beating on the fence with a stick. And this summer, these everlastin' peckerwoods have run my hogs to death.'"

"If you'll get your people grounded in the Word, they won't run after every religious peckerwood that comes through the country."

## On Abortion:

"Legalized abortion is nothing more nor less than legalized murder. The destruction of human life is murder by any measure. If that's shocking, I'm going to keep on saying it. We're living in a day when somebody's got to say something—God said that He placed me as a watchman, and if I see the sword coming and fail to warn the people, their blood shall drip from my hands—well, I'll not have bloody hands. I'm going to tell people the truth."

"The nation's unborn shall be there in the judgment. Up from the ash banks and the sewer pipes and the cisterns, there'll come nations unborn. Little feet that never prattled over the floor will find their way to the judgment, little tongues that never cooed 'mommy' and 'daddy' will find their way, little hands that never fondled and fingered your face will find their way to the judgment."

## On Revival:

"Do I think America is going to have a great revival? It is very necessary, if America is to survive. However, I see no evidence of it. I'm not looking for it for I feel that we're now living in the days of the apostasy. He said,

'That day shall not come except there come a falling away first' and 'When the Son of Man cometh, shall He find faith on the earth?' There'll be a famine, He said, not of bread and of water, but of the hearing of the Word of God. There is a famine of it today. You once went to church and listened to a preacher preach, you expected to hear a man who believed something. Today, if you go to a great many of the organized systems, you can't tell if the preacher is an infidel or a believer."

"I believe that's the reason God's blessing these great, independent, fundamental Baptist churches. But what's the remedy for apostasy? There is no remedy but judgment. They didn't have a revival in the days of Noah or there would have been no flood. I believe the only thing that would stay the hand of God is a revival of old-time religion. But we're rearing a generation of young people today who've never seen old-time religion. They've never seen an old-time, Heaven-born, God-sent, Holy Ghost revival. We need to realize that judgment is coming."

# Chapter 16

# SONS IN THE MINISTRY

B. R. Lakin was astute enough to realize that he was the last of the judgment preachers. Billy Sunday, Dallas Billington, Gypsy Smith, Howard Cadle, O. E. Caldwell and Homer Rodeheaver went to Heaven and left the preacher from West Virginia to remain behind. He often said, "I feel like an old stump in the middle of a beautifully plowed field—like I was born fifty years out of the harness." The world was changing and Dr. Lakin knew it, but he remained true to his calling, preached the Gospel, and never lacked for speaking engagements.

But he could not help but notice that he seemed to be the last of the old-time religion shoutin' preachers. When his son died, at first he lost all hope of passing on the mantle of his ministry. But then God led Dr. Lakin to a son in the ministry—Jerry Falwell.

Dr. Lakin once said, "Jerry, Mommy-Bob and I sort of look upon you as our boy because we lost ours."

Dr. Lakin began visiting Thomas Road Baptist Church about 30 years before his death. During his association with Falwell, Dr. Lakin learned to love and encourage the younger pastor and Jerry Falwell deeply appreciated his help.

"When I began getting involved in the social and political issues of this country about 10 or 12 years ago, Dr. Lakin would give me a lot of caution and instruction. He helped prevent me from going to the extreme in this direction or that direction. He'd say, 'Now don't run down a rabbit trail. That's a dead end. Stay on the main line and don't answer questions nobody is asking.' I got more education from B. R. Lakin than I ever did from all the schools I attended."

After Dr. Lakin's death, Jerry Falwell told a television audience: "In the last 30 years of his ministry, we crossed paths and he became my mentor, my teacher, the most

As he reached the age when many preachers retire, Dr. Lakin kept going. He began to speak annually at the Thomas Road Baptist Church, pastored by Dr. Jerry Falwell. The two became fast friends.

important human being in my life as far as the ministry is concerned. He hasn't been gone very long, and I miss him so much."

What began the relationship between the old country preacher and the controversial pastor? No one remembers exactly, but Dr. Lakin once said: "I think God put me in connection with Jerry."

Jerry Falwell was always grateful for that connection. In 1973, Falwell met with some of his darkest days. The Securities and Exchange Commission questioned the sale of general obligation bonds to finance the expanding national television and radio ministry and the new Liberty Baptist College. A Federal Court trial ensued. SEC officials wanted to lock the doors of the church.

During this time Dr. Lakin spoke at the church. He had been physically weakened by illness and was looking forward to a vacation after his engagement at Thomas Road. He spoke on Sunday, and on Monday he drove away. On Tuesday, after driving hundreds of miles home to Florida and back, he pulled into Falwell's parking lot. "Jerry needs me," he explained simply.

He was right. Jerry Falwell needed an encourager simply to talk, pray, and be with as he faced an uncertain future. Lakin spent the next four days with Falwell. He had the insight to realize that he was truly and deeply needed and the generosity to give of his time.

Several years after the two had been associated, John Rawlings once told Falwell, "Jerry, do you know where Dr. Lakin is valuable to you?"

"Where?"

"In 62 years, Dr. Lakin has never deviated from the fundamentals of the faith—come Hell, Heaven, or high water, he stays right on that. And he's never had a breath of scandal about him. When other people begin to knife you, one of them will say, 'Now listen, boys, he couldn't be all wrong, or Dr. Lakin wouldn't be with him.'"

Dr. Lakin not only protected Falwell by his association, but by direct action. He felt that God was calling him to provide a special influence in Falwell's ministry: "I started down there riding a mule with saddlebags and then I took the Cadle Tabernacle as one of my highlights, but now I think I'm in perhaps the closing glory of my meetings and of my ministry. I suppose what little I can do to help Jerry from time to time is what I'll be doing. He's the one that God has left as a prophet—that's holding high the Light and the Lamb in these days. And we ought to do as they did for another, we can at least hold up his hands, amen? I never go about the country, I don't go anywhere if they won't want me to do two things—preach the Gospel and talk about Jerry. You know if there is one thing I like about a preacher, it's a fellow that is not afraid to speak his mind and speak against sin. That's the reason I like Dr. Falwell. He's not a wishy washy 'Good Lord, Good Devil, You tickle me, I tickle you, Mary had a little lamb' preacher. That's not the kind of preacher he is. He's a man with a backbone and he preaches against sin."

"I think his greatest impact on the country is his stand for the funamentals of the faith and for the moral stand

Dr. Lakin preaching at Thomas Road Baptist Church.

in this country. No other pastor has been in a similar situation, because no other preacher has had the media to do what he has. I think he's doing what he ought to do and what he can do—I couldn't do it."

"But I don't try to be him. If I could only strike one note on the piano, it'd be 'B' natural."

Thomas Road Baptist Church began to invite Dr. Lakin to speak four or five times each year and he was always invited to co-host the annual "Super Conference" of the church.

When Mrs. Lakin's 94-year-old mother died, the Lakins carried her body home to the family cemetery in West Virginia. "We never dreamed of asking Jerry to leave his work in Lynchburg," recalled Dr. Lakin, "but he said he was coming to the funeral anyway. So he came up to our little country church and preached the funeral of that saint of God. I told him, 'Jerry, you're a big man. It takes a big man to do this.'"

Dr. Lakin had other "sons" in the faith as well. Bill Pennell first heard Dr. Lakin preach during a two-week meeting. He couldn't believe the emotional eloquence that poured from the foot-stomping preacher in the red bow tie. He had never heard the premillennial doctrine that Dr. Lakin espoused that night and Bill was determined to learn more about this preacher.

Bill went home and climbed into his attic for some papers that had belonged to his grandfather—another Baptist preacher. Amid the dusty pages Bill found several copies of *The Cadle Call* and read several columns by Dr. Lakin. He was impressed and wanted to know more about the preacher from West Virginia. The following years brought them together several times, and today Bill feels that it was Dr. Lakin who taught him how to preach and reach people.

During his lifetime Dr. Lakin felt that it was a priority to encourage and help other preachers of the Gospel. He loved to share what he knew and help young evangelists. Unfortunately, his concern was often met with ingratitude and/or petty jealousy. But Lakin understood human nature. "I don't have many friends," he once said. "Friends don't come in bunches like bananas. I have a little bunch and that's why I stay with them. If I leave the bunch, I'll get peeled."

Whenever he was emotionally hurt, he thought of Christ and His example: "One day He said, 'Why are you crying? I had some friends once. Twelve of them. They rode with me and watched me iron the wrinkles out of a raging sea, in a boat. They ate of the loaves and fishes from a boy's lunch that I provided for them. They saw me raise the dead and open the eyes of the blind—they saw all of that and yet one of them walked down across the little brook and over into the garden and said, 'Hail, Master' and kissed me. One out of twelve—you've got as good a batting average as I have, what are you crying about?'"

# Chapter 17

# LOOKING OVER INTO HEAVEN

**Just a gate open wide, and a friend by my side,**
**When I come to the end of the road.**
**That is all that I ask as a crown for my task,**
**When I come to the end of the road.**
**When the long day is ended and the journey is done,**
**I shall enter that blessed abode,**
**For the Saviour I love will be waiting for me,**
**When I come to the end of the road.**

As he preached and worked, Dr. Lakin was constantly aware of Heaven. He often remarked that his mother was praying, " 'Jesus, help my boy preach,' and old Bill, my boy, sitting up there is saying, 'Don't give up now, Dad.' "

In the last twenty years or so of his life, Dr. Lakin began to think more and more about his next home. When someone asked him if he was worried about dying, Dr. Lakin replied, "No, I'm sort of looking forward to it. Every now and then I tiptoe and peep and see loved ones in glory looking down at me. There is the morning as bright as day, Hallelujah."

"I'm often asked if I'm afraid to die. No, I'm not afraid to die, I've been to the water's edge three times and I've heard the waves lash against the boat, but I wasn't scared. Death is like an old bumblebee that Dr. Cadle once talked about. He and his brother, Cap, were out in the meadow and Dr. Cadle caught this bumblebee and cut off his stinger. He slipped it down Cap's overalls and laughed as Cap began to dance and slap himself. 'That ole bee can't hurt you,' he said. 'All he can do is buzz.' That's all death can do—just buzz."

Dr. Lakin told the Lord, "I want to stay here as long as I can and I'm going to keep holding on to the willows, but when the time comes, make it quick."

117

The trail began more than a million miles behind him, and Bascom Ray Lakin knew that it would someday end. "I do not know when, but one day it will come to an end down on the banks of the river of life. When they shove the ferry boat in and I step in, and step out on the other side and the captain of my salvation says, 'Old Soldier, it's time now for you to retire', I'll hang the sword on the shimmering wall of the city of God and hear him say, 'Well done, good and faithful servant. You've been faithful over a few things, I'll make you ruler over many.'"

"Heaven is going to be real. I think it's real today. I think if we could get on a missile and go out beyond the stars and the moon and all the rest of it, somewhere out yonder, we'd find Heaven. A big heaven, too. Fifteen hundred miles wide and long and high. I think that Heaven now is and will one of these days come down and be the capital city of the new Earth. Do I think there are people there? Yes, my mother is there and my daddy. Not with their bodies, but they're there."

Long before he arrived there, Dr. Lakin made his plans for heaven. "I think I'll go and sit down on the bank of the river of Life and dabble my feet in the water a few days, and then tell the Lord, if He doesn't mind, that I'll go back down yonder and preach some more."

"I wish I could sing—I always wanted to sing. But when I get to heaven, you wait. When my feet hit the shores, you will come out on the front porch of your mansion in glory and say, 'Dr. Lakin's come! I hear him singing.' And I'll walk out on the front porch of my mansion in glory and sing 'Amazing Grace, how sweet the sound that saved a wretch like me. I once was lost, but now am found, was blind but now I see.'"

"When I walk through the Eastern Gate of the Heavenly City, I'll ask someone 'Where are the hospitals?' 'They're gone. There's no sickness in heaven.' And I'll look around and say, 'Where are the hospitals for crippled children?' They'll say, 'We don't need any. There is no lameness up here.' And I'll look for the old folks homes, but they'll say, 'We don't have any—we don't get old in this land.' And I'll look for cemeteries—'We don't need any'—and for deaf people—'We don't have any'—and I'll say, 'Where do you go to church?' and they'll say, 'We go up to Jerusalem to worship the King.' And I'll go, and

I'll see the Lord high and lifted up in the holy hill of Zion and I'll hear the choir sing, 'All hail the power of Jesus' name, let angels prostrate fall. Bring forth the royal diadem, and crown Him Lord of all!' That's what I'm lookin' for."

"I don't know how long God will let me speak. But when He says 'Come', then I'm ready. I talked to a preacher who was eighty some years of age and he said, 'Doc, I'm just waiting, that's all.' I said, 'That's what I'm doing, but I'm working while I'm waiting. I think that is better.'"

On February 25, 1984, Jerry Falwell called Dr. Lakin at his home in Titusville. Dr. Lakin had been ill for over a year and had only been out of pajamas three or four times. Dr. Falwell said, "Dr. Lakin, you need to get out of that bed and come up here and preach for me."

"Well, if you'll send the plane down, Jerry, I'll try to do it."

Mrs. Lakin said, "I don't see how he can get up, Jerry, but I think it would be the best possible medicine for him."

His doctors agreed, and Dr. Falwell sent the plane down for Dr. Lakin. Dr. Lakin was carried onto the plane and the medics which Dr. Falwell had sent along took care of the prince of preachers who had been preaching 66 years—longer than Charles Haddon Spurgeon lived.

After his first heart attack the peppery old saint said, jokingly, "I have noticed that, if I make it through March, I'll make it through another year." He made it through that March, and many others, but on March 15, 1984, he died. Or rather, that was graduation day when Bascom Ray Lakin really began to live.

# Chapter 18

# LAKIN'S LEGACY
# AND HIS COMPATRIOTS

**Tho' much is taken, much abides; and tho'**
**We are not now that strength which in old days**
**Moved earth and heaven; that which we are, we are—**
**One equal temper of heroic hearts,**
**Made weak by time and fate, but strong in will**
**To strive, to seek, to find, and not to yield.**
*—Tennyson: Ulysses*

As the twentieth century nears its close, the Gospel remains changeless. But the manner in which preachers present the Gospel has changed dramatically. Today's preachers are concerned with social relevancy and problem solving; yesterday's preachers were concerned with judgment—"prepare to meet thy God." They relied upon the power of the Holy Spirit to bring about conviction and believed that you couldn't get a man saved until you got him good and lost. Lakin designed his sermons to bring about "compassion, conviction, contrition, and conversion."

Bascom Ray Lakin was the last of the giants. In an age when people flocked to hear fiery preachers with grand elocution and witty orations, Dr. Lakin stood toe to toe with the greatest preachers of the twentieth century. He was personally acquainted with Gypsy Smith, Billy Sunday, R. A. Torrey, Paul Rader, J. Frank Norris, and John R. Rice. He was always grateful that he "lived in the day of the giants."

Lakin had colorful memories of his fellow preachers. Of J. Frank Norris he said, "Now he was a fighting man. But I tell you what—I've eaten lunch with him, and he sat and talked about the Gospel and the tears just ran down his cheeks."

"Gypsy Smith was very tender, and Billy Sunday really

preached the Gospel. I've seen him walk that platform at Cadle and say, 'I ain't a modernist, God knows I ain't a modernist.' I saw him preaching one night on the Devil and he chased him up and down the platform and then ran over to the edge of the platform and kicked him off, and as he went down the alley, he spit on him."

Building dedication in honor of Dr. Lakin at Liberty University.

"And he prayed just like he talked. When he was shaving, you could hear him in there talking just like he was talking to you. I heard him pray one night in Charleston, West Virginia. He said, 'Lord, that delegation's come up here tonight from so-and-so and that man we've been praying about—' and here he called into the other room—'What's his name, ma?' she told him and he said, 'Yeah, God, that's the guy.' "

Dallas Billington was not only a fellow preacher, but

a close friend of Dr. Lakin's. "He was a great soul, and he was as clean as a hound's tooth. He had a way of preaching that had something on the end of it that caught you. And God used him. He was a great business man, he ruled the roost and was a great pastor."

Once Bob Jones Sr., Jack Hyles, Lester Roloff, and Lakin shared the platform at a meeting. Lester Roloff was preaching against the sins of television, but Bob Jones leaned over to the others and said, "I don't care what he says. I love Lucy, don't you?"

John R. Rice also preached for Lakin at Cadle Tabernacle. How was he? "Great," said Lakin. "Great exhortation."

According to Dr. Lakin, Dr. Torrey was a "logistician. Torrey stood up and spoke on 'because this happened, then this happens.' He reasoned from this to that. That's the reason Moody said to him, 'Wherever you preach, Torrey, and whatever you preach about, don't forget to preach a sermon on *Ten Reasons Why I Know the Bible is the Word of God.*'"

One of Lakin's best friends in the ministry was Homer Rodeheaver, a former associate of Billy Sunday's. Lakin especially admired Rodeheaver's walk with God. "Once I asked him about a song he wrote, *Forgive Me for Forgetting.* Rodey said, 'I was in a great First Baptist Church. I sang in the early services that morning. Then I sang in the Sunday school. Then I sang for the morning service, then I sang for the young people in the evening. And then I sang for the great evangelistic service Sunday night. Finally, at midnight, I was tired and worn and I went yonder to get on the train. I got on the Pullman, undressed, and then rolled quickly into the berth. But the voice of God said that I had forgotten to pray. And I asked the Lord to forgive me for forgetting.'"

Lakin considered Dr. John Rawlings to be his "bosom buddy", and he especially appreciated the ministries of Charles Billington, O. E. Caldwell, Jack Downs, and H. Frank Collins.

B. R. Lakin supported all Gospel preachers, whether they agreed with him or not. "If you can't tree the possum, don't shoot the dog that can," he believed.

How did Lakin regard his own preaching style? "Well, I don't know, I have a peculiar way of doin' it, I guess

I never was molded. I've got a mixture of all of it—I'm not original. The other day Billy Graham's magazine wrote me for permission to reprint some things from my sermon on *How May I Know There's a God*. I think I got an inkling of it from Torrey, but they wanted me to write and give them permission to use part of the sermon. So I said, 'Now, I don't know whether it's original; original is something you get and forget where you got it."

"My sermon is like a freight train. I can uncouple a few cars and kick around a few boxcars and hook her up and pull out and go on."

Though he did study for a short time at Moody Bible Institute, Dr. Lakin was largely self-educated. He trained himself by studying the Bible. Often he'd rise early in the morning and read the Bible on his knees. A verse he had been reading for years would suddenly reveal a new truth, and Dr. Lakin would be anxious for the chance to preach about it.

Like his compatriots, Lakin left a priceless legacy to those who followed him. Reviewing his life of preaching, Lakin said, "I have never knowingly done anything to bring a reproach or stain on the name of the Christ I love and who saved me. I'd rather die than live outside the will of God."

Among the many plaques which hang on his office wall, one reads "To Dr. B. R. Lakin: Happy Father's Day to the spiritual father of thousands with gratitude for 56 years of 'plowing, planting, and watering.'"

When asked how many were converted to Christ under his ministry, his quick reply was, "Oh, I don't know." Some say 100,000 is a conservative figure. Only eternity will reveal the number of men who were called into the ministry under Lakin's preaching and influence.

But Lakin's influence extended far beyond those who preach the Gospel. Bill Gaither, the well-known songwriter who has written such classics as *He Touched Me* and *The King is Coming*, cried when he heard the news of Lakin's death. "He pastored Cadle Tabernacle in Indianapolis, so as a kid, he was one of my first contacts with Christianity and the Lord. In fact, we got the idea for the song *It is Finished* from a sermon he had done."

The B. R. Lakin School of Religion is nestled among the mountains of Lynchburg, Virginia. Dedicated in 1982,

Dr. Lakin was honored to have a school bear the name of an "uneducated" country preacher: "This afternoon I stand here to say that as I walk back down the halls of memory, I stand again yonder at the forks of the creek in that little country church where I started preaching. I want to say this, no higher honor could ever have been bestowed upon me than you have here. I have never

B. R. Lakin preparing to go riding.

denied the faith. I believe the Bible today as simply as I did the day that I was taught it on a little Sunday school card. I'd like to think of this sometimes and say, 'Thy word, Oh God, is forever settled in heaven.' As far as I'm concerned, the Word of God is forever settled in Heaven. It may not be settled in some colleges, it may not be settled in some universities, it may not be settled in some seminaries, but in Heaven it is settled. I'll be coming back again from time to time and thanking God for this building and for those who will be taught the Word of God in it as the years come."

What advice did Lakin give to young preachers? "First of all, wallow in the Word of God. Second, learn to preach the Gospel—how Christ died for our sins according to the Scriptures. If you take long hair, short skirts, cigarettes, and Masons away from a lot of preachers today, they couldn't preach a lick. They'd be ruined. Don't chase rabbits, try to kill lions. Stay on the main line and preach the Gospel."

To young evangelists, he often said, "If you think that you're going to have a meeting one week and be at home one week, you'll never make it. If you think that you're going to jet out yonder, put your feet up in an air-conditioned Holiday Inn room and eat six dollar steaks, you're badly fooled. The churches that you're going to get to go to as you begin can't afford to do that for you. And you can't work only half the time and make a living. When you enter the church of a hard-working preacher, tell him to get you a room in someone's home. And tell him you'll go out to eat your own dinner. And if your wife wants you to be at home, you shouldn't have gotten married."

To young ladies, Lakin admonished, "If you're thinking about marrying an evangelist, you get ready to spend some lonesome nights and days. Go to work and do something, keep busy."

"If you're going to follow Him, it's not an easy road. But woe is me if I neglect to preach the Gospel; I've got to keep preaching and keep going. If you're going to have power with God, you're going to have to sell out to Him and put souls first."

"I've never asked, 'How much are you going to pay me?' I don't do that. I don't have any brochures or business cards—never expected anyone to write me anyway."

"Dr. Billington once invited me to preach a revival. He wanted me to come in on Friday, rest Friday and Saturday, and preach Sunday. Well, I preached Friday and Saturday nights, drove in, and was getting ready to preach Sunday morning. Dr. Billington said to me, 'You shouldn't have preached last night.' I said to him, 'If I hadn't preached last night, there's ten people who would have gone to hell—they got saved last night.'"

"If you want to know Jesus, be busy for Him."

# Chapter 19

# TESTIMONIALS

**Tom Malone:**

Dr. B. R. Lakin passed over the face of the earth for more than half a century, preaching constantly the Word of God and its message of life to unnumbered multitudes. No man can give of himself so long and so intensely, without learning much in the laboratory of human experience. Not only did B. R. Lakin have his soul forged upon the anvil of God's sovereign purpose, but he felt the heart throb and heard the soul cry of as many people as any preacher of this century. He walked among the masses and ministered to the needs of people. He was truly a tool which, though tried in many fires of the Lord's battles, always shone the brighter for Christ after conflict.

B. R. Lakin had no peer as a preacher. He was gifted by God with a brilliant mind and masterful eloquence. He was divinely endowed with an immeasurable amount of ability. All of this talent was completely dedicated to the service of the Lord Jesus Christ. I have often watched him take the Word of God and go to work on an audience as a skilled surgeon goes about his task. I have listened to him preach when it seemed that a heavenly halo had settled about him. I have witnessed God putting His stamp of approval upon this man as multitudes came to be saved and many lives were blessed and changed.

The many-faceted ministry of this man of God cannot be exaggerated. He has been the preacher's friend, the church's helper, the common man's leader and most of all, he has been for sixty-five thrilling, fruitful years,

God's mighty messenger. His sons in the ministry are all over America, and converts all over the world. What a God-send was his message, the voice of one of the truly great preachers of all time. As a preacher he had no equal; as a trusted friend, he was pure gold.

From the obscurity of the forks of the "Big Sandy" came this divinely-sent human meteor to pass among men and move them to Christ and His cross. As our generation speaks of Spurgeon and Moody and Sunday with loving admiration, if there be a generation before the Lord's return, it will lovingly speak of B. R. Lakin.

**Dallas F. Billington:**

It is extremely difficult to put into a few paragraphs the great love and admiration which I have for Dr. B. R. Lakin. It has been my privilege to have known Dr. Lakin for more than 40 years and in that time he has held more than 40 revivals here at the Akron Baptist Temple.

Dr. Lakin acquired many friends and listeners while a part of the Cadle Tabernacle at Indianapolis, Indiana. His many books of sermons are inspirational to all who read them. He is in my opinion, the greatest soul winner in the world today. His life has only one purpose and that is to preach Christ, never missing an opportunity to glorify the Lord.

Dr. B. R. Lakin is a pastor's friend and he understands the problems and needs of a pastor having pastored in many churches during the first years of his ministry. He is a true man of God and no sacrifice is too great for him if he furthers the cause of Christ.

**H. Frank Collins:**

The crowd overflowed the large drive-in theatre where Dr. B. R. Lakin was preaching the Gospel. The man by my side was an opera singer. As we walked away after the service he said, "When he preaches, I wish that I had never committed a sin against God."

I have seen the great city crowds fill the largest auditoriums and stadiums to hear this unique man of God from the hills in wagons, flat-bed trucks, and by foot to sit spellbound as this great preacher made God so real, Calvary so personal, and Heaven so near.

Although I am his son in the ministry, I stood as his pastor when we buried his only son high atop the West Virginia hills overlooking the peaceful valley that cradles the high log house that is home to this giant of a preacher who for years conducted "The Nation's Family Prayer Period" from Cadle Tabernacle on WLW. Here, too, his beautiful "Miss Bob" faithfully keeps the home fires burning, the radio mail answered, and the key ready to turn in the door to welcome home from his evangelistic campaigns God's great orator of the American pulpit for this generation.

**Harold Henniger, at the induction of B. R. Lakin into the Christian Hall of Fame, November 4, 1984:**
B. R. Lakin was born on a farm near Fort Gay, West Virginia. Although his parents were devout Christians, it was not until he was sixteen that he was converted to Christ during a revival. The minister who baptized him was the nephew of Devil Anse Hatfield of the Hatfield-McCoy feud families. One week later he preached his first sermon and soon after became a circuit preacher riding a mule to country churches near the forks of the big Sandy River. After attending Moody Bible Institute and pastoring several churches, he was called to assist E. Howard Cadle at the Cadle Tabernacle in Indianapolis, Indiana. Upon Mr. Cadle's death, he became pastor and during the next fourteen years the ministry grew until he was preaching to ten thousand people each Sunday in addition to broadcasting the services nationwide. He was given honorary doctorates by Bob Jones University and Kletzing College. In the early 1950's Dr. Lakin began a thirty-year itinerant ministry that included the largest churches in America, averaging fifty thousand miles annually and four thousand people weekly. He witnessed more than one hundred thousand conversions to Christ. His sermons were a combination of "sanctified wit," Bible teaching, and a strong appeal for people to "come to Christ." After more than sixty-five years of preaching, Dr. Lakin "hung his sword on the shimmering walls of the city of God" and went to be with the Lord on March 15, 1984. His funeral was conducted at the Thomas Road Baptist Church, Lynchburg, Virginia, and was attended

by more than five thousand people.

It was my privilege to have a part in that service. Today we honor him as we induct his portrait into the Christian Hall of Fame, bringing the number of portraits to 102. I think a fitting hymn to sing at this time would be "Faith of Our Fathers;" that is what he preached in the many, many revivals here at this church, and it is what we contend and stand for in this present hour.

(Dr. Lakin's portrait now hangs in the Canton Baptist Temple's *Christian Hall of Fame*, 515 Whipple Avenue, N.W., Canton, Ohio.)

**Don Norman:**

Dr. Lakin influenced my life in a great and wonderful way. He gave me insights into the Word of God that I've never known about, and he also made a lot of seemingly hard things in the Word of God very simple.

His real ability to move people and his knowledge of how to handle people was incredible. He could immediately capture an audience in the palm of his hand. He loved people, and wanted to help them, particularly young preachers. He saw the error of a lot of ways in young preachers and tried to steer them away from the pitfalls. He really spent a great portion of his life helping young preachers, and I appreciated the opportunity to watch him and learn from him.

## Chapter 20

# "IF THERE BE
# NO RESURRECTION"

On February 26, 1984, Dr. Lakin was present in the
service of Thomas Road Baptist Church. Dr. Jerry Falwell
asked if the old prince of preachers would like to greet
the people. "Sure I will," replied Lakin.

Knowing how weak Dr. Lakin was, Dr. Falwell offered
to stand beside Dr. Lakin, with his hand supporting him.
"No way," Lakin responded. "I'll just brace myself in the
pulpit and preach like I have so many times before."

The following is a transcript of his final sermon:

Thank you Dr. Falwell, and I'm very happy to be here.
The fact of the matter is, a man in my position is happy
to be anywhere. You wonder why Jerry is so marvelously
and wonderfully blessed. I'll tell you, he's been good to
the Jews. When you bless them, God will bless you. You
hurt them and God will hurt you. So I thank God for that.
I want you to continue to pray for him and for the success
of his work here.

I'm always glad when I have the opportunity to come
here and this will be my last place of coming. My wife
and I decided the other day that we'd come. Yesterday
we came up and Jerry asked us and said, "Why don't you
just come up for the week?" and I said, "Mommy Bob,
how about it?"

Dr. Lakin at the empty tomb in Jerusalem. He once said, "On my last visit to the Holy Land I was at the Mount of Olives and someone asked, 'Dr. Lakin, do you ever expect to come back here again?'" He replied, "Oh yeah, I'll be back, but the next time I come I'll be in the cavalry."

She said, "Sure," and I said, "Okay, that's good enough for me." We'll be here for the meeting next Sunday night. I want you to pray much for these meetings. I want you to pray much for Jerry. You know, I've been sick and down now for more than a year. I've only preached about three times and I get so now at night I can't sleep very well. So I was told to count sheep. I counted sheep until I got up to a million and then I found something else that did work. He said, "Just go over some of your old sermons you preached a few years ago."

And I started on one and didn't get halfway through it and I was sound asleep. That's the same thing that put him to sleep a long time ago.

Let me talk to you for just a few minutes now. We'll make it a few. I will talk to you for a few minutes on "If Jesus should never come back to this world. What would happen?" "Well," you say, "What does it matter?" Well, I'll try to tell you in about five or six minutes.

Jesus said, "I have the power to lay down my life and take it up again." He said, "They didn't take my life, I gave it. I had power to lay down my life and take it up again."

And he said, "Not only do I have the power to lay down my life, I have the power to pick it up." So His resurrection was within Himself.

You know about all I do in my preaching is to brag on Jesus. Just brag on Jesus. And I believe that if we do that, God will help us. So Jesus really went up to Jerusalem, was crucified, laid down his life, went down into the grave for three days and came out. Thank God, He came out and went out to the Mount of Olives with His disciples. On the way out to the Mount of Olives, He gathered them together at the top of the Mount of Olives and there gave His valedictory address. And as He was preaching, as He stood there speaking, in a moment His feet began to leave the earth. Slowly but surely, they looked in awe up beyond the trees and above the clouds and on into the blue. And as they stood gazing, He was gone.

Somebody said, "Is that all? We'll never see Him again, is that all? Will we never see Him anymore?"

He said, "This same Jesus that was taken up into Heaven shall so come again in like manner as you see Him go."

This same Jesus is not a mythical Jesus. This same literal Jesus was taken up literally into Heaven and will come back literally just like He went away—like He went away.

He said, "Well, what does it matter if He doesn't come back or not?"

If Jesus does not come back—if He does not come back, there never will be any resurrection. There will never be any resurrection of the dead for it is dependent upon His resurrection. But I believe He's coming in the same body that He went away in. I have a few things about the Scriptures that are a little strange to some of these fellas who are pretty heavy on works and know very little about grace. There's a lot of preachers that wouldn't know—they think grace is a girl's name.

Compare the unlimited favor of God to what I said—"if we pray long enough and act long enough and be the right kind of person long enough, we'll go to Heaven." That has nothing to do with it. Whether you go to Heaven or not depends solely on what Jesus Christ did upon the cross when He bought and paid for your sins. I'm going to get on you Baptists, some of you. Be a little bit more careful about that. Be a little bit more careful about praying the sinner's prayer. For God doesn't pardon sinners just because they pray a certain prayer. His forgiveness is granted on the basis of Calvary.

God doesn't forgive sinners upon confession. Listen, my friend, forgiveness means to let off without recompense so if the sinner could come up and beg like a whipped puppy and ask God to forgive him and God could wipe it away, then Jesus would never have had to die—if man was able to save himself. But he didn't.

That same Jesus that went up into the Heaven will come back again. Let me say this to you—

Well, suppose you sin after you're saved? Suppose nothing, I know you will. A man said to me one day that he hadn't sinned in 16 years. I told him I didn't believe it and he got mad. I knew he was lying then.

Why doesn't God whip these people? He doesn't whip people on my street that live like the devil yet they seem to prosper. I said, "Why do you get whipped?" If you're born again and saved, you're a member of the family and it's the members of the family that the Father whips. He chastens every son whom He receiveth. So my friend, you're saved and what are you going to do with these fellas who sin? They prosper and get rich and so forth. They'll get theirs later on. They're like a big hog that is getting fat for the hog killing. He'll get his out yonder at the end of the life. At the end of the age.

The moment I got saved, I came under the correcting hand of God. And His children, when they become members of the family He punishes them, He whips them.

That's the reason He doesn't punish the sinner now. Why? Because He doesn't go around whipping other men's children.

Let me tell you, my friend, there would be no permanent peace if Jesus did not return. There would be no binding of Satan if Jesus does not come. I believe he is going to be bound. I believe he is going to be bound, but he's not going to be by our works nor what we do. He'll take care of the binding. You'll never do it with Law. You'll never do it with law.

A couple got married and they had common sense. He said, "Now one of these days I'm going to come in and I've had a hard day. I'm not feeling very well. And I will tilt my hat. So if you see me tilting my hat on my head, you be nice to me. We'll get along."

She said, "Okay. But one of these days you'll come in and I've had a hard day. I'll have the corner of my apron pinned up, what then?" They hadn't made arrangements for that. He came in one evening with his hat tilted and she had her apron pinned and they hadn't made any preparation for that disaster. It's not by pinning aprons or tilting hats. It's by the calling out of the elect to complete the bride of Christ and the final resurrection— and then He'll come.

Because He is coming—and I'm as sure He's coming as I am standing on this platform—I can preach and labor and toil. But my work is not in vain. I know that I can bury my loved ones. I'll be buried myself one of these days. And when the heavens open, out of the heavens will come that one and the same Jesus that you see taken up into Heaven. He will come again in a like manner.

We were in Jerusalem once and stopped at the Mount of Olives. Somebody said, "Dr. Lakin, do you ever expect to come back here anymore?" Oh yeah, I'll be back. But the next time I come, I'll be in the cavalry.

On March 15, just seventeen days later, Dr. Lakin called his wife's hotel room at 6:30 a.m. "Bob," he said, "I'm ready to go home."

"Honey, we can't go home now," Violet answered. "You're too sick to travel. You need to stay and get better. When you're better, we'll go home."

"Whatever you say," the old preacher replied. And only minutes thereafter, the prince of preachers went home.

On February 26, 1984, Dr. Lakin preached his last sermon, "If There Be No Resurrection," at Thomas Road Baptist Church. He soon became ill and was hospitalized at Virginia Baptist Hospital in Lynchburg.

# EPILOGUE

"My life has been a miracle," Dr. Lakin once said to his wife. "I can't understand it. People come to hear me, and I don't know why they come to hear me preach, I just don't know. But I do know something—I'd rather die than be set aside. I'd rather die than to be outside the will of God."

# FAVORITE SERMONS
## OF
# B. R. LAKIN

# THE WOMAN
# AT THE WELL

There is no incident more touching in the life of Jesus than the conversion of the Samaritan woman at Jacob's well.

She was a typical sinner. First, because she had a hungry heart. She had found no satisfaction in the fleeting joys of earth. Her heart longed for the Water that would satisfy. She was a typical sinner also because she had a bad reputation. Her sins were flagrant and open; she was unashamed in her debauchery and wrongdoing. But she came to the well with an empty waterpot. This empty vessel symbolized the emptiness of her heart.

Let us consider this narrative in five divisions.

## I. THE CONVERSATION COMMENCED

*"There cometh a woman of Samaria to draw water: Jesus saith unto her, Give me to drink"* (John 4:7).

In speaking to this outcast woman of Samaria, Jesus was breaking all the rules of Judean etiquette. It was "taboo" for a Jew to carry on a conversation with a lowly Samaritan. But the love of Jesus knew no racial bounds, and He hurdled over this provincial barrier by engaging this weary woman in conversation.

I don't think that Jesus needed her help in getting a drink of water. He merely used this to strike up a conversation. This woman apparently had never before met

Jesus. She had never been interested in His life or activities. If she had heard about Him, her curiosity was not sufficiently aroused to bother to go where He was to see Him in person.

If all heart-hungry, lost men and women could just come face to face with Jesus they would feel differently about Him. This woman did not dream that He was so wonderful, so winsome, and so attractive. She had probably just thought of Jesus as another religious leader. It had never dawned upon her that He might be the long-expected Messiah. The conversation had not progressed very long until the Samaritan lady sensed that there was something divinely different about this person. There came a conviction to her that He was more than an ordinary Jew; there was a mystic air about Him that engaged her interest.

In answer to his command, *"Give me to drink,"* she said, *"How is it that thou, being a Jew, askest of me, which am a woman of Samaria? for the Jews have no dealings with the Samaritans."*

Then Jesus said: *"If thou knewest the gift of God, and who it is that saith to thee, Give me to drink; thou wouldest have asked of him, and he would have given thee living water."*

She had never had anyone speak to her about her soul. Men had been interested in her body for the purposes of sin. But this was something vastly different than she had ever known. Was it possible that somebody cared for her soul; she, a guilty, vile, scarlet woman?

The second step in the conversion of the Samaritan woman was:

## II. CONFIDENCE GAINED

In order to help an individual, you must first gain his confidence. Jesus, through this unprejudiced conversation, had been wending his way into her heart.

He told her of a water that was living, after the drinking of which one would never thirst again. Water is so plentiful in our land that we do not have the appreciation of it that the Orientals do. There are very few wells in Palestine. They have to be dug down hundreds of feet into the ground, and the water supply even at that depth is very limited. The idea of an artesian well springing up within, so one would never thirst again, sounded almost too good to be true.

After Jesus had gained her confidence by dealing gently and kindly with her, she finally said, *"Sir, give me this water, that I thirst not, neither come hither to draw."*

These were the words that Jesus had been waiting for. He was a master salesman of eternal life. He knew the human heart: what it needed and what it desired. Now this lady was ready to sign on the dotted line and accept this Living Water. But there were a few things to be considered before she was to partake of this new life. Jesus said, *"Go, call thy husband, and come hither."*

She blushingly replied, "I have no husband!" When the power of Christ comes into a life it affects your home relationships, and this woman's home life was bungled and confused. She had been a woman of many husbands, so Jesus struck at the very heart of her need when He said to her: *"Thou hast well said, I have no husband: for thou hast had five husbands; and he whom thou now hast is not thy husband."*

Christ knows all about you. His all-seeing eye can penetrate the darkest closet of your past and see every skeleton hidden there. The fact that Jesus knew about her past, and still was willing to be seen talking with her, moved her deeply.

## III. CONSCIENCE REACHED

The Holy Spirit of God enters the human heart through the portals of the conscience. There must be a remorse for sin before there can be the seeking of a Savior. When the convicting power of God comes to a life it is like good medicine—it sometimes makes the patients feel worse before they feel better.

We often sing and speak of the comfort of Christ, but sometimes He makes us feel awfully uncomfortable. I am sure that the words of Jesus about the Samaritan woman's past did not make her very happy. For a moment she was chagrined and embarrassed. But this misery was turned to music when she acknowledged Him as her Savior and Messiah.

If Saul had never been pricked in his heart, he would never have known the joy of salvation and had his name changed to Paul. Conviction is the growing pain of the Spirit.

"Blessed are the poor in spirit" has always been hard for me to understand. But some Bible scholar pointed out that it literally means: "Blessed are those who are conscious of their spiritual poverty."

The Samaritan woman in the presence of Christ felt lost and undone. She suddenly became conscious of how poor she was spiritually, and she was quick to acknowledge it. Standing by Jesus, she felt as Isaiah did when he stood in the presence of God and said, *"Woe is me! for... I am a man of unclean lips."* But when an angel of God came down and touched his lips with a coal from off the altar, he caught the missionary spirit and said, *"Here am I; send me!"*

## IV. CONVERSION EFFECTED

*"The woman then left her waterpot, and went her way into the city, and saith to the men, Come, see a man which told me all things that I ever did: is not this the Christ?"* (John 4:28-29).

The big thing that she had done was to recognize Jesus as the Messiah and acknowledge Him as her Lord. *"Believe on the Lord Jesus Christ, and thou shalt be saved"* is the clarion call that rings down through the centuries.

But there were two or three evidences of her conversion.

1. *She Left Her Waterpot.*—This symbolized the old, empty life she had lived. She had received the living water; the old life had been supplanted by the new. When a person finds Jesus the life is changed. As Paul said in II Corinthians 5:17, *"Therefore if any man be in Christ he is a new creature: old things are passed away; behold, all things are become new."*

2. *She Became a Witness for Christ.*—*"Come see a man which hath told me all things."* She had come in contact with the One who is altogether lovely. He had changed her life, and she was not ashamed of Him.

The early church grew rapidly because everyone in the church was a witness for Christ. When Peter preached his sermon on the Day of Pentecost there were three thousand conversions. But Peter should not have all of the credit, for there were one hundred and nineteen other disciples who were witnessing to the truth which he was preaching.

We talk Christianity and we argue it with our friends, but there is very little real witnessing today. The Samaritan woman had a real testimony and clinched it with an invitation for others to find Him and to know Him.

3. *She Brought Her Friends to Christ.*—*"Then they went out of the city, and came unto Him."* The townsfolk knew this woman. She was notorious. She had no doubt been a problem to the community. Of all the people in the town she was probably the most irreligious. When she came running into the city, yelling, *"Come see a man, which told me all things that ever I did: is not this the Christ?"* they were astounded and amazed. Her speech had never been religious before. She was never seen in the Temple or the synagogue. So they knew that something unusual had happened to her.

Her message was: "Come, see a man." They were so impressed with the change in her life and her sincerity that the record says, "Then they went out of the city, and came unto him."

Christians are afraid that they will offend their friends if they invite them to Jesus, but we owe it to them to give them one challenge and invitation whether they resent it or not. When we have made an effort to lead them to Christ, then their blood will not be on our hands.

## V. A CHANGE MANIFESTED

When the world sees that our testimony rings true and that our lives have been transformed and changed, then what we say will be more effective. The reason the gospel of Christ is not "selling" today is because there are not enough genuine samples of Christianity. The world would rather see a Christian demonstration than to hear a Christian discourse. Samples, not sermons, are needed; changed lives, not cheap lingo; possession, not profession. When the worldly crowd sees salvation at work in the lives of men and women they will take knowledge of us and be attracted to Christ.

The Samaritan woman offered her "changed life" as an example of what Christ could do, and the whole city "came unto him."

*The skeptic cannot change my mind;*
*Tho' millions turn from Christ away;*
*They cannot tell me He is dead;*
*For I just talked with Him today.*
                              —L.C.F.

And when we convince the world that He is real, that
He can change our lives, and that he gives us the happiness
for which the human heart craves, then our churches will
be filled with people seeking Christ, and righteousness
will cover our nation as the waters cover the sea.

# HOW MAY I KNOW
# THE BIBLE IS THE
# WORD OF GOD?

*"These things have I written unto you that believe on the name of the Son of God: that ye may know that ye have eternal life, and that ye may believe on the name of the Son of God." I John 5:13.*

The discussion of this vital question, "How may I know the Bible is the Word of God?" is of vital importance to all of us. The matter of our soul's destiny rests entirely upon our attitude toward the veracity of God's Word.

If we carelessly regard it as "just another book," "a collection of ancient events and stories" or as a compilation of allegories, we rule out our chance of finding God through its precepts. Or if we fall into the tragic category of those who dare to scoff at the Bible, saying it is nothing but myth and fable, we make ourselves worse than the devils, who believe and tremble before the unchangeable truth of God's Word.

Our disposition toward the Word of God then becomes a focal point upon which the question of our eternal destiny is centered. How could any sane, thinking, intelligent person regard this question lightly? It is certainly one of the most important questions ever put to mankind. So we are on sacred ground; let us tread reverently, reasonably and logically as we discuss this question, which to many may be a matter of life and death.

Before we get into the foundational statements of our message, I suggest that you lay aside all preconceived notions you may have about the Bible. If some college professor, taking advantage of your immature mind, dared to scoff at God's Word and the seed of doubt was planted in your brain, I suggest that you remove this accumulation of mental cobwebs and approach the subject of the moment with an unprejudiced, open mind.

If our educators would learn to stick with education, the field in which they are trained to serve, and keep their noses out of religion, about which many of them know little or nothing, our students in our colleges and universities would come back home with more faith in God. My motto is: "Let the church promote Christianity and leave education to the educators, and let the educators promote education and leave Christianity for the church to interpret." A teacher has no more right to express his personal religious whims and fancies in the classroom than a preacher does to drag dirty politics into the pulpit.

So I feel that I am right in my department today in bringing you this message on the Bible, the Word of God.

I offer seven suggestions by which we may know the Bible is the Word of God:

## I. THE ANTIQUITY OF THE BOOK

*"But the word of the Lord endureth forever. And this is the word which by the Gospel is preached unto you."* I Peter 1:25.

No other book has survived the centuries unaltered as has the Bible. The very fact of its existence at all is the greatest proof of its being the Word of God. It has survived empires, kingdoms, civilizations, wars, the dark ages, the Renaissance, modernism, skepticism, the old deals, the new deal and all of the raw deals that have been perpetrated against the race.

It has successfully withstood the verbal onslaughts of such champions of unbelief as Payne, Voltaire, Ingersol, Darrow, Maribeau, Marx, Nietzche and Mencken. It has outlived the books written by its opponents and will survive the writings of the present crop of disciples of doubt. Moreover, it will continue to shine in all of its luminiferous brilliance upon generations of humankind yet unborn. For this matchless tome says of itself:

*"Heaven and earth shall pass away, but my words shall not pass away."* Matthew 24:35.

Voltaire, in the zenith of his popularity, said: "The Bible will be a short-lived book." Soon after he spoke those cynical words he went out to meet the God he had defied. The world soon forgot the frivolous words of the clever Voltaire. In recent years a few of his admirers have made a frantic effort to revive his writings, but all in vain. And ironically enough the very house in which he lived was purchased by the French Bible Society and is used for a storehouse for Bibles. All of this is in literal fulfillment of that portion of scripture which says:

*"The grass withereth, the flower fadeth, but the Word of our God shall stand forever."* Isaiah 40:8.

When Professor Curie announced the discovery of radium, men marvelled at its ability to impart energy without the loss of strength. But for centuries the Word of God has imparted its strength and power to countless millions of men, and yet its influence and energy have never diminished.

The theories of men are faddish and changing. Styles change, systems change, governments change, the world maps change; everything about us is transient and shifting, but the Word of God remains unaltered. It is the one fixed value upon which all other values are based. It is the one criterion by which all true standards are measured. It is the universal standard by which all human justice is measured.

Scientists tell us that the sun is growing cold. Disturbing changes are taking place in the celestial sphere. The Bible goes further and says that some day the moon will turn to blood and the sun will be darkened. Earthquakes will change the topography of our globe and, according to II Peter 3:12, ... *"the heavens being on fire shall be dissolved and the elements shall melt with fervent heat."* Only one thing will remain unchanged, and that is God's Word! This is the sure foundation upon which the child of God shall stand when the material world and shifting elements vanish away.

So I know the Bible is the Word of God because of its antiquity. It has weathered the stormy past of time. It has outlived the centuries. It stands undaunted and unchallenged. Verily, as David said: *"FOREVER O LORD*

*IS THY WORD SETTLED IN HEAVEN."* Psalms 119:89.

Secondly, I know the Bible is the Word of God because of:

## II. THE TRANSFORMING POWER OF THE BOOK

*"For the Word of God is quick and powerful, and sharper than any two-edged sword, piercing even to the dividing asunder of soul and spirit, and of the joints and marrow, and is a discerner of the thoughts and intents of the heart."* Hebrews 4:12.

No other book possesses the power to transform life. What drunkard was ever made sober by reading Shakespeare? What libertine was changed into a saint by the reading of Milton or Keats? What liar was ever made truthful by reading Payne or Voltaire? What selfish tyrant was ever beaten into humble subservience by the reading of Byron or Burns? What hypocrite was ever made holy by the reading of Ingersol or Maribeau?

It stands alone on the highest pinnacle of respect and admiration and is recognized by the most brilliant minds of the ages as the only book that can work the miracle of "change" in the human heart and personality.

Saul, the apostate, was changed into Paul, the beloved apostle, by the magic of its power. Luther, the "bull," was transformed into the angel of the reformation when the light of its truth dawned upon his soul. Moody, the "shoe clerk," was changed into Dwight L. Moody, the "soul merchant," when its truth struck his heart.

What piece of literature other than the Bible can change a hovel into a home? What other book contains the mystical chemical power to change alcohol into shoes, stockings and groceries? What other power in the world can wrest a human soul from the brink of Hell and transport it into the realm of other-worldliness?

It makes the proud humble, It makes the poor aware of his riches in Christ. It makes the capitalist love the laborer and it makes the laborer have regard for the capitalist. If its power was unleashed in the world, it would put an end to strikes, disputes and riots, and the human family would at long last live in peace and tranquility.

This book takes the fraud out of politics and its power in the life of a politician takes him out of fraudery. It creates due respect in the hearts of men for their fellows and causes a rebirth of the scriptural truth, "NO MAN LIVETH UNTO HIMSELF."

It is a boon to the human family, a benediction to the individual and a blessing to all who embrace its truths and teachings. Its panacea is a healing balm, its precepts morally stimulating and its commandments universally adapted to the needs of the race.

It supplants hatred with love, avarice with generosity and bigotry with kindness.

An African native came running to the missionary compound much disturbed. He cried, "Oh, my dog, my poor dog! He will be no good for the chase any more. He is spoiled for hunting."

"What on earth happened to your dog?" inquired the missionary.

"He ate part of my Bible and it will ruin him for hunting. When I got the Word of God in me it made me love my enemies! My dog won't chase the game any more, he's ruined," lamented the native.

Many people object to the effectiveness of the Bible on the ground that it is outmoded and obsolete.

The Bible is an old book, but it doesn't follow that it is obsolete. The multiplication table is old, but not obsolete. Nothing has ever been devised to take its place in mathematics.

The alphabet is old, but not obsolete. Modern teaching methods have tried to manage without it, but we have come up with a generation that can hardly spell.

Honesty, kindness, truthfulness, courtesy and friendliness are old, but not obsolete. Things should not be discarded simply because they are old. The reason some things have endured the centuries is because they are eternally worthwhile and useful.

This leads me to say that I know the Bible is the Word of God because of:

## III. THE UNIVERSAL APPLICATION OF THE BOOK

*"I am not ashamed of the Gospel of Christ for it is the power of God unto salvation, to the Jew first and also to the Greek."* Romans 1:16.

Most books are written for a particular group or class. But the Word of God adapts itself to the needs of all men.

Its truth applies equally to civilizations past, present and future. Men of every age have been challenged by its message, convicted by its precepts, inspired by its noble teaching, comforted by its promises and moved by its power.

No other book has been translated into as many languages. It lends itself to free translation and is equally understood by people of all races. It has now been translated into more than 700 languages.

It was not written exclusively for the German people and yet it has claimed the attention of such German greats as Luther, Barth and Boehller. It was not written exclusively for the Italians, but it was the staff and guide of such Italians as Savanarola and St. Francis. It was not written exclusively for the Englishman, but it was the transforming agent in the lives of such men as Wesley, Whitefield and Calvin. It was not written exclusively for the Jews, but it was the staff of Moses, the life force of Paul and the guide of the early Jewish Christians.

It is not a one-man book, a one-nation book or a one-race book, but it is one book that meets the needs of all men.

Confucius and Buddha appealed to the oriental mind with their philosophy, but their teachings have never been accepted universally by the people of the world.

Darwin, in his "Origin of the Species," appealed to the occidental, materialistic mind, but his philosophy has never been accepted by the Orientals. But the Bible possesses a universal appeal and its message speaks to the needs of every race.

Charles Darwin once visited the aborigines who inhabit the vicinity of Cape Horn at the southern tip of South America. The natives resented his theories and teachings and he barely escaped with his life.

Sometime after that, Thomas Bridges, the British missionary visited Cape Horn, armed only with his Bible and the Spirit of God. The natives readily accepted his message of redeeming love, and today there exists in that quarter of the world a high state of Christian civilization. The Bible had once more triumphed over the philosophies of man, and the universal application of its message had been demonstrated once more.

It is the Bread of Life to the hungry; a Guide for the

lost; Healing to the sick and afflicted; a Light to those in darkness; a boon for the poor; a blessing to the rich; and the one indispensible book for all men of all times.

It is found in the humblest home and in the most luxurious hotels. It is appreciated and esteemed by scholars, scientists, philosophers, authors, and world leaders. And yet it is so simple that missionaries are able to interpret its message to raw heathens in a few minutes.

Kings, presidents and public speakers rarely ever address their audiences without quoting from its pages. And yet its precepts are quoted by the countless thousands who do not have the benefit of school learning.

Children lisp its holy words as they bow at their mother's feet, and great and mighty men utter quotations from it with their last dying breath.

Again, I know the Bible is the Word of God because of:

## IV. THE SCIENTIFIC ACCURACY OF THE BOOK

Although the Bible is not a text book of science, its statements are in strict accord with true science; the infidels not withstanding.

Listen, "alec smart," if you are so cock-sure about the Bible lacking scientific accuracy, I'll tell you how to make some money. A Christian businessman in Chicago has deposited $1,000.00 in a Chicago bank and will give it to the first person who can prove that there is one statement in the Bible contradictory to true science. So, if you are so positive that the Bible is full of errors, why don't you collect the money? I know why you don't, and you know why you can't—the Word of God can stand the acid test of scientific scrutinization and has done so across the centuries.

Ancient materialists believed that the world rested on the back of a huge turtle, and that the turtle stood on the back of a large elephant, and that earthquakes were caused by the elephant shaking himself. But the Word of God says in Job 26:7: *"HE HANGETH THE EARTH UPON NOTHING."* These words were spoken centuries before man discovered that the earth was suspended in space and was held there by a mysterious power called The Law of Gravity.

A little over two centuries ago, scientists discovered that the blood cells of the body contained the living organisms which perpetuate human life. They were praised for their great findings by the people of the world and modern medicine is based upon this fundamental theory. But little did these scientists know that the Bible 5,000 years ago declared this scientific truth, just 4,800 years before they found it out. In Leviticus 17:11 it says: *"For the life of the flesh is in the blood."*

In the 14th century, it began to dawn upon men that the earth might be spherical in shape instead of square, as was previously supposed.

Christopher Columbus and others spent much time and vast amounts of money in the effort to prove that it was round. The world slowly but surely accepted this truth. But the Bible, 500 years before Christ, revealed to mankind that the earth was round when Isaiah said in the 40th chapter and 22nd verse: *"It is He that sitteth on the circle of the earth and the inhabitants thereof are as grasshoppers; that stretcheth out the heavens as a curtain and spreadeth them out as a tent to dwell in."* Here Isaiah not only revealed the shape of the earth, but hinted as to the orbits of the heavenly bodies and their circuitous path.

Time would fail us to note the accurateness of the Scriptures in scientific data, but suffice it to say that the Word of God reveals more and has revealed it longer and more accurately than any scientific text book ever devised by man.

Just a few years ago, liberal professors laughed and scoffed at the idea that Moses wrote the first books of the Bible. They contended that written language was unknown at that early day in history and that, consequently, the Bible was a mere compilation of legends and fables gathered throughout the centuries, and that there was no authentic proof of its inspiration.

But the most recent findings of archeological authorities have turned the laugh on these presumptuous skeptics and have proved beyond the shadow of a doubt that the history of legible writing goes back farther than Moses.

The "Tel Amarna" letters unearthed by modern archeological experts is a group of 320 missives from Egyptian consuls in Palestine to Pharaoh and his officials in Egypt regarding business and political conditions in the Holy Land before Moses was born.

Archeology has verified the accurateness of the Biblical account of antedeluvian history. Life during the Pharaohs has recently been proved to be exactly as the Bible describes it.

For example, in the fifth chapter of Exodus, God says that Pharaoh ceased giving the children of Israel straw to reinforce the bricks they were making for his cities, and he compelled them to use stubble instead. But finally, he forced them to make the bricks without any stubble. In 1908, Professor Kyle excavated and examined the ruins of the old city of Pithom, one of the cities the children of Israel were used in building. He found that the lower courses of brick were made of clay and straw, and that the middle courses had stubble. But the upper courses had neither straw nor stubble, thus proving the accuracy of this remote and seeming unimportant incident. But these findings of science proved once more that the Bible is indisputably correct, even in little details.

Another reason I know the Bible to be the Word of God is the literal:

## V. FULFILLMENT OF ITS PROPHECIES

The Word of God and the history of man combine to prove the inerrant accuracy of the prophecies of the Bible.

Prophecy is the recording of events before they happen. It is history written in advance. The history of the race was pre-outlined in HIS-STORY, the Word of God.

The Bible deals with the ultimate rather than the immediate. It speaks of the destiny of the earth; the fate of the earth people; it speaks of a new Heaven, a new earth, and a new life. It begins before man could begin and carries on long after man has finished.

The foreknowledge of the Book is intangible proof of its inspiration.

In Genesis, the Bible speaks of the seed of the woman which would bruise the head of Satan. Jesus came as the "seed of the woman," and His coming, His death, His resurrection bruised Satan, the head of the powers of evil. He conquered death, Hell and the grave and brought life to those who were under Satan's spell of death. He literally bruised the head of Satan.

The Bible prophesied that Jesus' own people would

reject Him. It foretold every detail of His death, His betrayal, His burial, His resurrection and His ascension. More than 100 prophecies about Jesus, the Messiah, were accurately fulfilled at His coming.

The Bible prophesied the fall of nations, and they fell. It prophesied the conditions of our day. *"Many shall depart from the faith ... and the love of many shall wax cold."* ... *"False prophets will arise."* ... *Nation shall rise against nation."* ... *Iniquity shall abound."* ... *"And there shall be wars and rumors of wars."*

The Bible prophesied the return of the Jewish people to Palestine. *"But the Lord liveth, which brought up and which led the seed of the House of Israel out of the north country and from all countries whither I had driven them, and they shall dwell in their own land."* Jeremiah 23:8.

We cannot take the time to consider this great truth longer, but there are hundreds of fulfilled prophecies which history authenticates and human experience corroborates, which convince the logical mind that the Bible could be none other but the Word of God.

I believe further that the Bible is the Word of God because of the:

## VI. UNIVERSAL RESPECT FOR THE BOOK

On the radio networks we have been hearing the announcers saying: "Read the Bible daily; it is a reliable Guide, and the law-book of the world!" What other book is shown such respect and given such prominence? It speaks well for our American way of life that such an announcement is permitted on the airways. It helps one to believe that in this day of seeming despair that there is still hope for our civilization, for as the Word itself declares: "Righteousness exalteth a nation, but sin is a reproach for any people!"

The Bible is the world's best seller and has been for many years. Printing presses are working overtime to meet the demand for copies of the Word of God.

The longest cablegram ever sent was transmitted October 21, 1881. It contained 180,000 words. It was the King James translation of the New Testament. Within a matter of a few hours, 36 compositors set the type, and the printing presses started rolling, and 20,000 copies of the New Testament were printed in New York. Within

24 hours, every copy had been sold, and people were clamoring for thousands more. This only proves again the universal respect people have for the Word of God.

It has found its way into thousands of hotel rooms through the splendid work of the Gideons. Testimonies have come to them of how the Bible has saved men from suicide, from lawless living and from moral collapse. Its power is unchanged; its appeal undiminished and its truth unaltered.

We have seen the effectiveness of its power as we have proclaimed its unsearchable riches. Literally hundreds of people have written in to tell us of how they were saved from taking their own lives and plunging over the abyss of moral despair, through the truth of God's Word and the power of the Book. We thank God for the privilege of proclaiming it. I wouldn't trade places with the President, or with the King of a great empire. We wield a mightier sword than they, "The sword of the spirit which is the Word of God."

And last, I believe the Bible to be the Word of God because of the:

## VII. THE CENTRALITY OF THE BOOK

Is it a book of beauty? Yes, but much more. Is it a book of science? Yes, but much more. Is it a book of poetry? Yes, but much more. Is it a book of history? Yes, but much more. Is it a book of law? Yes, but much more.

IT IS A BOOK WITH LIFE-GIVING PROPERTIES! AND THIS LIFE COMES FROM ONE WHO IS THE CENTRAL PERSONALITY OF THE BOOK.

Every book has its leading character and the Bible is no exception. He is seen in Genesis with God in creation: *"All things were made by Him and without Him was not anything made that was made."* His reflected image is clearly visible in the pools of sacrificial blood upon the altars of ancient sacrifice. He walks in type through the dramatic narratives of the Old Testament. His form becomes more visible as Isaiah describes Him saying:

*"He was wounded for our transgressions; He was bruised for our iniquities; the chastisement of our peace was upon Him and by His stripes we are healed."* Isaiah 53:5.

At long last He came IN PERSON to sojourn with man. He came in the tender body of a little babe. The "daystar" had appeared. The world took on a sacred glow. The blind received their sight. At His Word, the lame walked; the lepers were cleansed; the dead were raised; the burden of sin was lifted; the long night of darkness was o'er. The light of the World was shining upon mankind.

The Bible was written of Him, and for Him, and points mankind to Him. He is the center, the core, the very heart of the Word, and every page of the Holy Book is illumined with the sacred light of His presence.

If you do not see Him in the Book, you have missed the purpose of the reading of it. If you do not find Him there, God's intent and purpose has been lost, and the hope of your Salvation is gone. It points the Way, the only Way, and if we ignore its precepts, transgress its law and reject its Christ, there is no hope for us in this world nor in the world to come.

When the elements melt with a fervent heat,
    And the earth-things shall all pass away;
When the gold and the silver have lost their worth,
    And man's work is lost in decay.
When the end of all things has come at last,
    And time shall have come to an end;
What will the hope of your heart then be?
    WHAT WILL YOU STAND UPON THEN?

I have a hope that is steadfast and sure;
    And I fear not the gathering storm;
I have an Anchor that holds me secure;
    And I look for the crisis to dawn.
I have a Saviour who stands by my side;
    "I'll be with you," He says, "to the end,"
So, when all things of earth are fading away,
    I'LL STAND ON HIS PROMISES THEN!

The storm clouds are coming, that Day is at hand;
    When the Lord shall return for His own;
The trumpet will herald that glad command,
    When He gathers His saints 'round the Throne.
Will you then be counted in that great throng,
    Who trusted His grace to the end?
Will you stand with Him, or all alone?
    WHAT WILL YOU STAND UPON THEN?
                                            —L.C.F.